CONQUER THE
CLASSROOM

*"How to Manage Your Students,
Your Administration, and Yourself*

ROBIN REED RIGGLE, B.F.A., M.ED.

BOOK DOMAIN LLC

Literary Agent Endorsements:

Alex Glass, Literary Agent
"Conquer the Classroom" is a thoughtful and compassionate guide that doesn't just identify the pain points educators face—it offers real, practical strategies to reclaim control. Robin Reed Riggle brings both insight and authenticity to a field that desperately needs her voice. This book should be essential reading for educators, administrators, and anyone who wants to thrive in the education system today.

Amy Brewer, Literary Agent
Robin Reed Riggle writes with the heart of a teacher and the wisdom of a veteran. Her book is empowering, inspiring, and most of all—actionable. "Conquer the Classroom" is a powerful reminder that educator wellness is not a luxury; it's a necessity. Riggle's strategies helped me rethink what teacher success looks like, and her voice will be a lifeline to countless educators.

Daniel Lazar, Senior Literary Agent
This book is timely, fresh, and deeply necessary. Robin Reed Riggle has written a smart and emotionally resonant guide to surviving and thriving in the classroom. I was impressed by her holistic approach—balancing classroom management with personal wellbeing—and her natural gift for motivating others to act. "Conquer the Classroom" is the kind of book that doesn't just inform, it transforms.

Laura Wood, Literary Agent
With an empathetic voice and years of hands-on experience, Robin Reed Riggle brings real-world solutions to an overwhelming profession. Teachers will find themselves nodding in agreement, taking notes, and—perhaps for the first time in a long time—feeling hopeful. This is more than a how-to book; it's a movement for sustainable teaching.

Rebecca Sherman, Senior Literary Agent
"Conquer the Classroom" is the antidote to teacher burnout that we've all been waiting for. Robin Reed Riggle seamlessly weaves her 18 years of teaching into an inspiring and approachable framework for restoring joy and purpose to the profession. If you've ever loved teaching but lost yourself in the process, this book is your roadmap back.

Audience Reviews:

Harvey Slater, Holistic Nutrition & Wellness Coach, Author: *The Thrive Handbook*

In "Conquering the Classroom," author and public school teacher Robin Riggle generously shares her experiences navigating her career through an extremely difficult time in not only her career but in the broader teaching profession. Her personal story about her stumbling into a social media post discussion that landed her on administrative leave, followed by her brave commitment to defend her reputation and career, winning her hearing, and then reinventing herself in a new classroom setting will be valuable for any educator in today's climate who is feeling discouraged, dark, and alone in their quest to fulfill their mission of bringing knowledge to young people. Robin follows up each chapter with brief words of wisdom and 'bullet points' to help the reader navigate the challenges that come with the job, allowing them to 'conquer the classroom' in a holistic, empowering way, rooted in self compassion and connection to one's own truth and integrity.

Niranda Wanthivanond (Nida), Retired Preschool and Elementary School Teacher of 38 Years

Conquer the Classroom by Robin Reed Riggle is a heartwarming and inspiring nonfiction book that is both easy to read and thoughtfully written. In this short yet impactful work, Robin shares her honest experiences from her work life, personal life, and spiritual journey. Through her storytelling, she offers readers meaningful and compassionate suggestions for both professional and personal growth. One of my favorite features of the book is the "Seeds to Grow On" section at the end of each chapter. These thoughtful challenges encourage readers to reflect and take positive steps forward, making the lessons feel both practical and uplifting.

Patricia E. Van Osterhoudt, M.A., Postsecondary Learning and Reading Specialist

Classroom teaching can and will consume you, if you let it. This is why Robin Riggle lends her years of teaching experience to you with compassion for those moments when you are lost in the deep forrest of education. In Conquer the Classroom, Robin reshapes the hard edges of academia by giving each of her readers time to reflect with self-love on the challenges both life-changing and small daily adjustments in one's teaching life...

Jeannine Dole, B.S., M.Ed., High School Teacher & Instructional Coach (36 Years)

This is not just a book on teaching, it is a story, a cautionary tale, and a helpful guide for teachers, woven together to make for a very interesting and educational read not only for all teachers— but especially for new teachers. Robin not only shares her horrendous and extremely stressful tale of how social media and seven little words almost destroyed her career, she also shares how to protect yourself —both emotionally and spiritually—when taking on the world's most important job, that of being a teacher.

Nancy Sirski, M.A. Ed., Superintendent/Principal Mt. Baldy Joint Elementary School District (Retired)

On the surface, Ms. Riggle's book serves as a timely cautionary tale for students, educators, and administrators navigating the complex demands of the virtual world. But at its heart lies something deeper: a powerful, deeply personal account of Robin's journey through adversity. Through challenge, introspection, and unwavering faith, she emerges with a renewed sense of purpose, hope, and redemption...

Toni Blackmon, Classroom Teacher for 35 years

"Conquer the Classroom: How to Manage Your Students, Administration and Yourself" by Robin Reed Riggle has genuine pearls of wisdom for teachers. Her experiences in teaching and going through challenging situations really resonate... Ms. Reed Riggle's personal experiences, battles with depression, anxiety, and the eventual triumphs she endured make this a must read for teachers.

John Norvell, Ph.D., Professor of Anthropology, Mt. San Antonio College

This elegant and heartfelt little book is an expansive and generous take on a favorite teacher motto: Don't let the turkeys get you down. Built around a harrowing account of an administrative injustice of the kind that would drive some from the profession, Riggle's book does not dwell in outrage, but rather gives us a multifaceted and inspiring reflection on how to find and keep joy in a life of teaching.

Lisa Cook, Classroom Teacher (1992 – Present)

To build on the metaphor Grow Where You Are Planted, Conquer the Classroom provides the nourishment for cultivating a healthy balance between personal and professional life so that the reader can "plant" healthy practices that will grow into a fulfilling career... Reading the court transcripts opened my eyes to what district administration was capable of and how little support teachers have...

Rhiannon Wamsley, Substitute Teacher and Photographer at Cosmic Zen Photography

Robin's book feels deeply personal and honest. All throughout, it's as if she's gently guiding me, hand in hand. Her vulnerability and respectful tone shine through as she shares her own detailed experiences... There is true value in her knowledge and anecdotes that I will always remember moving forward.

Pat Montague, Language and Reading Specialist; Consultant for Rigby and Harcourt Publishers

Riggles tells a poignantly descriptive story of how a single misinterpreted group email totally upended her career and personal life. Past successes and knowledge by the administration that she was a very caring teacher never entered the equation, as a hasty, "no questions asked" decision was made to interrupt her dedicated teaching...

Mrs. Ikzury Paneto, Middle School Math Teacher

Robin Reed Riggles's Conquer the Classroom speaks directly to the heart of a teacher. As she describes the challenges and rewards of teaching, she stirs and tends the soil of the heart. Her "Seeds to Grow On" are planted in my being and remind me that growth is a process...

Jessica Reed, Contributing Writer for Guideposts Magazine, Chicken Soup for the Soul Books and The New York Times

Teachers hand out textbooks at the start of each school year with stars in their eyes and a steadfast belief in the unlimited potential of each and every student entrusted to them... Conquer the Classroom is a self-help formatted, hybrid memoir... detailing the author's legal fight to defend her beloved career and recover her sense of self. Riggle breaks the fourth wall and directly addresses the reader in a conversational tone that feels like an empathetic friend.

Linda Sanchez

As a fellow educator, I highly recommend Robin's book. It is practical, insightful, and delightful. A must-read for all educators in the ever-changing classroom!

Rebecca Park, ELA Teacher, PhD Candidate

A Must-Read for Educators at Every Level Robin Reed Riggle's "How to Manage Your Students, Your Administration, and Yourself" is a refreshing, insightful, and highly practical guide for educators navigating the ever-demanding world of teaching. With a voice that is both compassionate and authoritative, Riggle offers a well-balanced blend of real-world strategies, personal anecdotes, and research-based techniques that empower teachers to thrive in all aspects of their professional lives. What sets this book apart is its holistic approach. Riggle doesn't just focus on classroom management or administrative relationships—she skillfully addresses the full ecosystem of education, including the often-overlooked element of self-management. Her sections on maintaining personal wellness, setting boundaries, and cultivating resilience are especially valuable in today's high-pressure educational climate. Riggle encourages collaboration and communication, offering tools to build mutual respect and understanding between teachers and administrators. Her strategies are grounded in experience and clearly come from someone who has walked the walk. For classroom management, Riggle goes beyond the standard tips and tricks, helping educators understand the "why" behind student behavior and equipping them with the tools to foster a respectful, engaging, and productive classroom culture. Whether you're a new teacher just entering the field or a seasoned educator looking for renewed inspiration and practical tools, this book delivers. It's accessible, encouraging, and full of wisdom that's immediately applicable. Robin Riggle has given educators a valuable resource that feels like a supportive conversation with a trusted mentor. I could not recommend this book more!

Closing Note:

Conquer the Classroom has already begun changing lives. These endorsements—verbatim and unsolicited—showcase the heart of a book with the power to uplift and transform. Robin Reed Riggle is not only an educator but a voice of clarity, compassion, and resilience in a world where teachers need encouragement and practical tools more than ever.

We thank you for considering this remarkable work for publication and would be honored to speak further about the growing interest it continues to receive.

Benjamin Lopez
Literary Agent

All inquiries should be addressed to:

Book Domain LLC.
543 E Louise Dr Phoenix, Az 85050

Ordering Information:
Amount Deals. Special rebates are accessible on the amount bought by corporations, associations, and others. For points of interest, contact the distributor at the address above.

Printed in the United States of America.

ISBN-13	Paperback	978-1-967903-20-7
	eBook	978-1-967903-19-1

Library of Congress Control Number: 2025910878

I dedicate this book to my daughter, Ashley. You are my sunshine and before you were even here, you challenged me to be the best version of myself, each and every day.

"For a seed to achieve its greatest expression, it must come completely undone. The shell cracks, its insides come out and everything changes. To someone who doesn't understand growth, it would look like complete destruction."

— CYNTHIA OCCELLI, AUTHOR OF
RESURRECTING VENUS

CONTENTS

ROOTED IN LOVE

"Empathy:
Let me hold the door for you.
I may have never walked
A mile in your shoes,
But I can see that
Your soles are worn
And your strength is torn
Under the weight of a story
I have never lived before.
So let me hold the door for you.
After all you've walked through,
It's the least I can do."

— MORGAN HARPER NICHOLS

Dear One, I see you! I know that you are the first one to arrive on campus, so you have plenty of quiet time to prepare for the demands of your teaching day ahead. You are such a thoughtful, loving, and kind wife, mother, sister, daughter, teacher, neighbor, and friend. Each person who crosses your path in life comes away from the encounter feeling seen, heard, and loved.

Your day always starts so early, waking before the sun even thinks of peeking over the horizon. Many times, you are awake even before your 4:45 a.m. alarm starts demanding your attention. Sometimes I see you pull the covers back over your head, especially in the cold and dark of winter, wishing you could fall asleep for just ten minutes more. You know the backward math and calculate that you cannot stay in bed one more minute. Your clothes are already hung on the back of the bathroom door so you don't have to switch on the blinding light and wake your husband.

You lovingly prepare lunch for him and your two teenagers before you leave for work. Your husband will get breakfast for your kids and get them off to school, but your daily lunch prep is your way of letting your family know that they are loved, nurtured, and cared for. It's your way of centering yourself for the day, silently making the sandwiches and wrapping the fruit, chips, and cookies in love and prayers for the day—letting them all sleep just a tiny bit longer.

After your breakfast of coffee with cream and yogurt with blueberries, you make sure your car is packed and ready for the hour-long commute to school, mentally checking each item off: laptop, lunch, teacher bag, coat, purse, travel coffee mug. Quietly, you tiptoe back into the house to kiss your daughter, son, and husband goodbye for the day, grateful you have the family of your dreams. They are your light, love, and joy—your very reason for being.

As you make your way to work, I see the way your thoughts shuffle through the obligations of the day. The car glides through the freeway traffic almost automatically as you mull over points you want to make in that I.E.P. meeting at 8:00 a.m. Hopefully the sub understands the lesson plans you hastily wrote for second period math so you could attend the meeting. As a high school teacher, you have so many students to connect with and worry about—150, give or take. You hope you are meeting their needs and that they feel nurtured and supported.

You suddenly remember that it is your turn to bring the sliced oranges to your son's soccer practice tonight, so that's one more errand to add to the drive home in a schedule that's already stretched to the limit. You think it's a good thing you graded those essays from fifth period last night, as your students will need them for revisions today. So much to juggle, think about, and organize! With any luck, you'll get to school early enough to make the photocopies for period six and not have to do it during your already short lunch. You pull into the faculty parking lot into your favorite spot near your room. Loading all your stuff in your arms, you make your way to your class in one clumsy trip. Yes! There's just enough time to run to the office and check the mailbox before the bell for first period rings. The donuts look tempting, but you think of the Friday date night with your husband and decide to pass on the empty calories.

How do I know these things about you? I've walked miles in your shoes and worn the different hats—daughter, sister, mother, wife, neighbor, teacher, friend. I know that each and every one of these roles is so important to you and you want to excel in them all. Sometimes it seems that there just aren't enough hours in the day to get all that's expected of you crossed off the ever-expanding list. Someone needs to invent a time machine to insert more hours into the day! It makes me exhausted and stressed out just to think of all the things jostling for attention in my brain.

I know that becoming a teacher wasn't the career you dreamed of when you were young. Instead of studying art and writing and illustrating children's books like you planned, your parents steered you in the direction of something more practical and dependable: teaching. After all, they did pay for your college education, so they got an important voice in the matter. You decided on a degree in special education, since there is just about always a demand for that wherever you look for teaching jobs. It has been a good career for you, blending in nicely with raising your kids and spending time with their grandparents, aunts, uncles, and cousins, who all live nearby. Family is so important to you and at least you don't have to work nights, weekends, holidays, or summers (or so everyone thinks!).

Anyone intimately involved with a teacher knows the blood, sweat, and tears we pour into teaching and taking care of our "kids," as we lovingly refer to our students. It is in our nature to want to do our best for them and help them all reach their full potential. Actually, it is a joy and a privilege to get to work with kids. It's awesome when things are going as planned and your students are excited, engaged, and doing well with a lesson you worked so hard to prepare. It's even better when it fits in perfectly with all the state standards and it just so happens to align with your upcoming required observation.

It's always great to get good feedback from the administrators and have them recognize all that you are doing to serve the varied needs of your students. It's wonderful when things are sailing along smoothly but it certainly takes trial and error and lots of experience to make it look effortless. And it doesn't take much to have it veer off course—a phone call at exactly the wrong moment, a snide comment by a student, or pencils flying across the room when you are writing something on the board. You can't let your guard down for a minute. You are the captain of the ship, steering all those souls across the seas of self-discovery.

The one key element that is so important is building relationships with your students, including getting to know them and their names as quickly as you can. That can be a challenge, especially at the start of a new school year. With changes and adjustments made to schedules, sometimes your classroom can seem like a revolving door. It eventually settles into a rhythm and each class begins to show its own unique personality: chatty, super-serious, funny, frustrating, endearing, inquisitive, and more.

My dear, sometimes in life we think we know what the plan is, but the Universe has other ideas of where our lives are headed. It might be that our path in life naturally flows from us, based on our experiences. I know that you would have loved to study art in college but sometimes we make a choice that seems like a sacrifice at the time, then it actually ends up being for the greater good in the long run. Think of your students and the families whose lives you positively impacted. You taught them all how to be patient, kind, loving, supportive, and curious about the world around them. You have shown them how to believe in themselves. By stepping up to the plate, embracing your career as a teacher, and getting your master's degree, you modeled dependability, personal growth, and action that benefits the entire family to your own two children. Your kids saw you and your husband working as a team, taking turns making dinner, and chauffeuring them to sports practices to support you getting your degree. It's certainly not easy doing graduate level work while teaching full time and raising busy teenagers. But you did it and continue to do it with grace, poise, and professionalism.

I see you wanting to excel in everything you do. Being a great wife and mother is the most important job in the world and you wouldn't trade it for anything. Being a great mom naturally influences how you teach, and your students can feel how you genuinely care for them as if they were your own. Most of us who became teachers did so because we truly love being around kids and want to help them become the best versions of themselves. There is something so sweet and endearing about working with students who might be a bit reluctant at first, then once they realize you are there for them (even on days when they're not at their best), they jump right in and give it their best for you. That is the rewarding part, when you have a student who keeps you up at night, worrying how you might better reach them, and they make that shift and begin to believe in themselves.

You have to cherish those little moments and tuck them away for later when you need a bit of joy and encouragement yourself.

That is the fun and rewarding part about teaching—when you start building upon those relationships, gaining students' trust, and helping them to really grow into who they are meant to be: rooted in love. I'm about to take you on a journey, the story of how, despite plans of my own, I became a teacher.

My friend, we both know that teaching comes with many challenges and rewards. It is in our nature to contemplate these things. As I wrap up each chapter, I have included "Seeds to Grow On" summaries, to reflect on while reading, as you grow personally and professionally in your journey as a teacher.

SEEDS TO GROW ON

- *Carve out space* when and where you can work uninterrupted so you can focus with intention. Before or after school are ideal times. Set a time limit and go home when the time is up.

- *Connect with your family and friends* in meaningful ways, even if the gesture is small. As my mother used to say, "Good things come in small packages."

- *Don't be afraid to delegate* to family, students, and colleagues, sending the message that you uphold your boundaries. That way, your work energy is targeted on your most important tasks.

GROWING INTO
A TEACHER

"Too often we underestimate the power of a touch, a smile, a kind word, a listening ear, an honest compliment or the smallest act of caring. All of which has the potential to turn a life around."

— *LEO BUSCAGLIA*

Dear One, as you think about your teaching, I want you to remember what called you to this work in the first place. Think back to how excited (and nervous) you were when you were setting up your first classroom of your very own. You created every space in the room to welcome and invite your young scholars into your community of learners.

As a teacher, it is fun to be on the giving end on the spectrum of life-long learning. As a child, I loved books, learning, discovery, and going to school. I didn't always want to be a teacher, though. My mother was an excellent teacher and taught first grade for over thirty years. Being the oldest daughter of a preacher and a teacher, my sister, brother, and I were raised in a loving, fun, and supportive family. I saw how hard my parents worked to give us a happy childhood. We were rooted in love and our family life revolved around the dinner table and the lively conversations we shared, where each and every topic was up for thought-provoking discussion. At home, my mother was always working on one project or another for school. I saw how much work went into being a great teacher and that wasn't the direction I wanted to go. I was free-spirited and creative and spent my afternoons riding my Schwinn varsity bicycle up and down the Southern California coast.

Having way too much fun and losing focus on my education at C.S.U., Chico, I became a college dropout in the mid-80s. It wasn't until I met my husband, Alan, and we had our daughter Ashley, that things started falling into place, leading to me becoming a teacher. Eight years after dropping out of college, being Ashley's mom made me want to set a good example for her and go back to finish college. We started at C.S.U., Fullerton when she was fourteen months old for two reasons: they had an excellent children's center where she could go while I was in class, and they had a great art department. So, off we went to college. I secretly worried that I was singing the Barney song (I love you, you love me) out loud as I made my way across campus to my art classes. I finally earned my Bachelor of Fine Arts degree by the time Ashley was six and a half. My class ring actually says, "About Time," since the word "illustration" was too long.

As Ashley made her way through our little K-8 Mt. Baldy village school with its eighty-five students, I spent a lot of time there as a parent volunteer. Our principal, Dr. Tenpenny, suggested I should be a teacher's aide since I was there so much. As I gained more confidence and experience in the classroom, I decided to get qualified as a substitute teacher. As Ashley progressed through the grades, so did I, eventually making my way to substitute teach in schools down the hill, too.

I loved being around the kids with their eagerness and excitement to learn new things. By the time I had subbed for six years, I decided that I wanted to teach in my own classroom. Love was the root of it all: a love for the students and a passion for art. So, I was going to get a single subject teaching credential in art and become a high school art teacher. There's kind of a running joke that if you want to be an art teacher, you have to wait for someone to die or retire. I was determined and told God that I'd get the credential if he got me the job. Within one week of finishing my credential at the University of La Verne, I got the art teaching job at the one and only district I had applied.

It's amazing how God's perfect timing continues to show up in my life when I follow my heart and His gentle guidance. I got the confirmation I needed that I was in the right place when I got a phone call from our family friend, Beth, one afternoon in June of 2007. We had known Beth and her husband, John, and their family long before Alan and I were married. Actually, their daughter Lisa caught the bouquet at our wedding. Alan and John had known each other for years, working in the building trades together.

When Beth called, she explained that she had the wrong phone number for us, but she'd been trying to call me for a month. She was excited to tell me that her school district had an art teacher opening, a rare occurrence, and she wanted to make sure I knew about it. When I asked her what school district she worked in, her answer somehow didn't surprise me. Instead, I felt like an invisible hand was gently clicking gears inside me into place. The feeling almost took my breath away. I told her that I had just been hired by the very same district. When we have the faith that things will work out and do our part to create success, life definitely works in mysterious ways. With that, Ashley and I started our separate high school adventures together in the fall of 2007.

Right when I began teaching, I began a teacher journal that helps me to remember golden nuggets I've gathered along the way. In no particular order, it is filled with snippets of my days—the good, the bad, and the ugly. It has sweet notes of thanks from appreciative students. There are tiny drawings students have given me, or those I've rescued from the trash that are much too adorable to throw away. There are moments when the student becomes the teacher and I have something to learn.

Early in my high school teaching, I had someone who kept turning in assignments with the student name, Verga Sanchez. When I'd call out the name to hand the paper back, all the students would laugh. I just assumed that Verga was absent that day. After a couple times of this happening, a shy young student handed me a note on his way into class one day. It was folded up really small and he whispered for me to read it later and never tell that he wrote it. His note said in tiny letters, "Verga means penis."

Needless to say, I never got to meet my invisible student, Verga Sanchez. I get a chuckle every time I come across that helpful language lesson. My teacher journal even has some hastily written venting poems that have captured some of the more frustrating moments in teaching. We've all had those moments where a student has done something so outlandish that you are thinking to yourself, "I wish I could walk out the door, right in the middle of this class period, get in my car, drive to Palm Springs, and never come back!" Of course, you never do leave, but the thought definitely crosses your mind.

You can't have thin skin when you are a high school teacher and eventually you learn to take it all in stride. You hear bits and pieces of conversations never meant for your ears as you walk around the room. I flick my finger by my ear, saying, "Delete, delete, delete," with a smile on my face as I continue on my rounds.

It's fun to find different ways to connect with your students and one great way I've done that, as an art teacher, is to play music for them during class. I've shared many favorites with them over the years and had students introduce me to artists they like, too. That was one good thing about having a high school age daughter while I was teaching high school. Ashley would often make me CDs of her favorite songs and my students loved them. Playing music lightens the mood in the room and creates a natural segue when I turn the music off to share a certain point about art or let them know it's time to clean up.

As you gain skills and confidence in your teaching and classroom management, it shows you are a team player when you are willing to take on leadership roles on campus. Take it in baby steps to make sure you are not overextending yourself and that it fits into your family responsibilities. For example, before our daughter Ashley learned how to drive, for two and a half years, I took her down the hill to high school and picked her up as well. She was in cross country, soccer, and track and had practice after school most days, so I felt comfortable in taking on the extra responsibility of photo and art club advisor at my high school, as I had plenty of time to grade assignments while I waited for Ashley to finish practice. I teased her that I sometimes felt like I lived in my car at the parking lot of her school.

When we are in the midst of raising our kids and teaching our students, we sometimes feel like we'll be doing this forever—especially on days that are hard or frustrating or nothing seems to be going right. You have to teach yourself to be in the moment and find little things to appreciate or be grateful for. As your daughter or son graduates from high school and goes off to college far away, you'll look back and realize how quickly it all flew by.

So, my advice to you is that when you are in the middle of all the hectic chaos—packing lunches, grading papers, planning lessons, attending all the sporting events, commuting on the freeway, getting dinner on the table—stop! Look around you. Memorize the moments. You'll be so glad you did. That's what life is made of: one small moment of now, happening again, and again, and again.

SEEDS TO GROW ON

- *Make time for professional growth:* once you feel confident in the day-to-day management of your classroom, stretch just a bit past your comfort zone. Volunteer to sponsor an after-school club or a museum field trip.
- *Make time for spiritual growth:* Read a daily inspirational passage, meditate, go for walks. Do some yoga poses and deep breathing, even if it's just in your classroom between class periods.
- *Make time for social growth:* Make a standing date with a family member or friend. Try something new once a month.

3

UPROOTED IN AN INSTANT

"Sometimes what didn't work out for you really worked out for you."

— *UNKNOWN*

Oh, sweet teacher friend of mine, I see your heart and soul, for we are kindred spirits. Even though you put on a brave face and maintain a cheery disposition, I see your undercurrent of despair, your weariness, your tiredness to the bone. I know you work so hard to meet everyone's expectations, but you are leaving someone important out of that equation: *yourself!*

We all have things that keep us up in the middle of the night exactly when we should be resting, replenishing our souls. We toss and turn, seeking elusive sleep. What about Johnny in period three who just doesn't want to try? I know your parents are healthy now but they're getting up there in age and you hope it stays that way. What about your own kids? Your students take so much of your time and energy. You worry about whether or not you are being a good mom. I know how you feel, like you just don't think you have the energy to teach another day. Let me tell you a story of a time like that for me...

February 17, 2017 started out like all the countless days before, waking before the crack of dawn to get ready for another stressful day of teaching. Little did I know, that day would be the last day I'd ever be teaching in my high school classroom. Don't get me wrong. There were plenty of things I loved about teaching art to my students at the Southern California high school, an hour-long drive from my home in Mt. Baldy village. I loved to challenge my kids to do their best, even if they thought the assignment was hard. I loved for them to learn how to express their own unique creativity. I loved greeting them all at the door with little, "How ya doing?" conversations as they boisterously spilled into the classroom.

I loved to encourage them to make friends while they were making their art. Hearing their laughter as they chatted and drew, while we all listened to Bob Marley or mix CDs my daughter, Ashley, had made, was music to my ears. I loved to display their art in my huge classroom and see their excitement as they admired the latest displays. I was blessed to have such a great job, sharing what I learned about art and life with my students as they learned to navigate the world. But lately, the behavior of some of the students started to become more challenging. Things like pulling out their cell phones—not allowed in class on our campus—and refusing to put them away. It was hard to maintain composure and continue calmly teaching the other thirty-five students as one of them cussed me out.

Just three weeks before, on the Presidential Inauguration Day, January 20, I had a shocking racially-motivated fight in my classroom. A Black girl and a Mexican girl badly beat another Black girl who was brand new to my class and our district just the day before. On my way across the room to call the office, I whispered to the girl being vulgarly taunted, "I'm getting you help."

She bravely did not retaliate and sat on her hands with a tear rolling down her cheek. The two girls vaulted across the room and pinned the young lady to the ground, punching her in the face. There was a sickening "thwack" as her head hit the concrete floor. It took two phone calls and six adults to get help and break up the fight. A couple of students even jumped up on desks and started chanting, "Fight, fight." The on-campus deputy mistakenly tried to handcuff the girl who had been the victim and I had to tell him to stop. It was my worst day teaching ever! Some days, the sciatic pain from the stress was so bad I could hardly get into my car at the end of the day.

On February 17th, preoccupied with the day's lesson about Pablo Picasso and mixed media techniques, I noticed butcher paper on the wall outside my room.

We were getting ready to make Picasso inspired self-portraits in class. First period had gone pretty well, as I walked around with my sample of techniques to share with the kids. Second period felt a little weird though, as students who were normally friendly and talkative entered the room silently, staring right past me as if I were invisible.

I was walking around the room trying to get the kids involved with the sample making when I heard a key in the door. In walked two people from the District Office, introducing a third gentleman, they said, "This is Mr. So and So and he's going to watch your kids for a few minutes while we go up to the office and talk." There was a stony silence with the exception of footsteps echoing on concrete as we marched to the office.

When we got there, I asked if I should have union representation with me and they brushed it off as not being a disciplinary issue. Then they asked me if I had anything in my classroom that I needed. Not thinking of my ten years' worth of lesson plans, teaching materials, books, movies, music CDs, life drawing costumes, and still-life props, I just said, "My lunch, my teacher bag, and my wool coat." They went to get my things, asked for my keys and I.D., and told me to go, saying I was on administrative leave.

Not wanting to go near my own classroom, I walked past the front of campus, noticing for the second time that morning that several walls were covered with more butcher paper—something I'd never seen before. I later learned the tagging was so obscene and racist that it needed to be covered immediately.

As I neared my car, one of my teacher friends bolted out of her classroom and chased me to the parking lot, giving me a huge hug. She explained that a Facebook post we six teachers had commented on the day before had gone viral and been seen more than 20,000 times, about "The Day Without an Immigrant!" There was even a reporter from the Washington Post who left a message waiting for me at home. The February 16th day of protest was really meant to bring attention to all the contributions that immigrant workers added to our national economy.

Finally understanding the nature of the administrative leave, I thought back to the Facebook post. I disagreed with our colleague who made the original Facebook post about the day. Not wanting to judge him, I steered the conversation in a more positive direction, or so I thought. At home on my own computer, I added my observations of the day. I had fifty absences. We had a pleasant day. Thanking my friend Briane, I made my way to my car. Too stunned to even cry, I started my drive home in a daze. Once off the freeway, I pulled over and called my husband, Alan. Bursting into tears, I told him I couldn't drive up the mountain and asked if he'd come meet me down the hill.

Being on administrative leave in the year that followed was one of the darkest times of my life. The day we six teachers were escorted off campus, a riot broke out at our school, spilling out into the community with students marching, chanting, and jumping up onto news vans. We received national media attention—and not in a good way. We each faced our own hearings before different administrative law judges. The things the school district said about us were soul-crushing. They labeled us "immoral, dishonest, and unfit to teach." Being called a racist bitch on Facebook and worse hurt me to my core.

That wasn't how my brother, sister, and I had been raised. Our parents, a minister and a teacher, taught us to be loving, kind, and supportive of all people. We often shared dinner table conversations where any and every topic was up for a lively debate, and each person's point of view was valid. I was a good teacher, and I loved my students, putting my heart and soul into working with them. I volunteered for extra things like photo and art club advisor, WASC focus group leader, chaperoning trips to museums, South Korea, New York City, and Washington D.C. Earning a master's degree, I created a bilingual survey to ask my students and their parents about the importance of an arts education, wanting to better serve our mostly Hispanic community. I was doing my very best and always got great evaluations from my administrators. I won my case, but the school district appealed my win. Continuing with the litigation, I still won my case and the district didn't quite know what to do with me. They said they would never put me back at my high school.

Four days before Christmas of 2017, the same lady from the district office who had taken me out of my classroom called me at home. That surprised me, as all communications with the school district were supposed to come from my lawyer. She said I won my case, and I was to report to the middle school in our district in January, 2018, on the same day the students returned from winter break.

Middle schools in our district did not normally have art classes, so they needed to create a position for me. A few days before I was to start at my new school, I did a test drive to see where it was (six miles closer!) and how long it took me to get there. The place was deserted with the exception of one person. Dressed in jeans, I thought perhaps he was part of the custodial staff. The campus was locked, and he was behind the gates.

Seeing me, he walked over and introduced himself. He knew exactly who I was because he was head of the technology department for the district and he testified against me in my case. I could barely breathe, and my heart started beating faster. He seemed friendly enough and said that he had worked with middle schoolers before, and I'd do just fine.

But I had such a visceral reaction to the fact that he was part of the group of people who had said such horrible things about me. I went straight home and literally was sick in bed with fever, chills, and vomiting for three days. With barely any prep time, I had to dive right into teaching a younger group of kids, seventh and eighth graders. During my substitute teaching years, that was the age group that was the most challenging to me. After the hearings that I endured, I really didn't know if I even had the courage to ever teach again.

However, there ended up being many blessings to my new teaching position at the middle school in my district. From the moment I walked onto campus, my union-involved colleagues welcomed me with open arms, even though they knew what happened to me at the high school. For the first time in ten years, I was getting enough sleep since my junior high students started school at 9:00 a.m., instead of the 7:10 a.m start time at the high school. The winters used to be especially hard when I'd have to leave home in the dark and get home when it was dark, too.

My new school had a garden and I got to grow flowers and veggies and even have fun with my students doing beautiful pastel drawings of the garden outdoors. My mom, who taught first grade for over thirty years, gave me the best advice, saying, "Robin, be sure to eat lunch with your teacher friends." At the high school, I always invited my students and their friends into my room so that anyone would have a safe and welcoming place to be. I followed my mom's suggestion though, and from the start, shared lunch, laughter, and stimulating conversation with my new teacher friends on campus at the middle school.

Fast forward, and I have been at the middle school for two and a half years. I've gotten better at teaching seventh and eighth graders. I love their creativity, conversations, laughter, and dedication to trying their best. With the coronavirus pandemic, we have all had new challenges to face with learning to teach remotely. Since we couldn't have our usual student art show on campus, Carol, one of my teacher friends, helped me post our first ever virtual art show on Instagram.

Even though I loved my job at the high school, despite all the mounting stress, I probably would have never had the courage to leave. My mom and dad were my greatest supporters throughout this whole ordeal.

My dad was one of three people chosen to testify on my behalf in my hearing. My mom's cheery advice to me as I started all over again was, "Bloom where you are planted."

I even used that as an idea for a "start of the year" art project. Each student got to illustrate a favorite plant or animal. Together, we created a beautiful garden wall, with contributions from each child, encouraging them to grow, starting where they already were. All along, I think God knew exactly where he wanted me to grow too.

So, you see, Dear One, life can get pretty dark sometimes. You can feel so full of despair, but God is orchestrating things in the background that we could have never imagined for ourselves. Just breathe and be. Take the time to nurture your soul. It's when things seem to be falling apart that they are really just reorganizing themselves, making way for new and better ways. You just have to trust in the process and keep moving in a forward direction, even if it is just one step at a time.

You are enough, just the way you are.

SEEDS TO GROW ON

- *Be mindful of what you share online.* Maybe sharing an after school Starbucks with a colleague would be a chance to debrief or vent. Remember to be respectful of student privacy and not use any names in public.
- When faced with challenging times remember *the sun is still shining* behind the clouds. Take a few moments to write five things that are going right in your life, despite the troubling times.
- Be open to allowing change in your life. If something is not working and it is a constant struggle, perhaps there is another way, even if it's just a shift in perspective.

4

DRAGGED THROUGH THE MUD

"Darling, you're not falling apart, you're getting rid of the pieces that no longer serve your purpose. This is surgery of the spirit and it can be painful as hell."

— *KALEN DION*

I know what you're thinking, my friend: "Life is not so neat and tidy." Horrible, immobilizing situations just don't get resolved in a day and then wrapped up brightly with a bow. In the aftermath of the Facebook fiasco, I felt like I was living in some sort of Twilight Zone alternate reality.

Shunned by my peers, silenced, and isolated, I felt like my reputation was being dragged through the mud. In my heart of hearts, I knew I was a great teacher but that was not the feedback I was getting, and I started to doubt myself. Immediately, the six of us involved in the questionable Facebook thread were locked out of our work email accounts and access to student records.

It was time for our first progress report of the spring semester and I was concerned about getting my report card grades in on time, as I hadn't yet entered all of my student grades into the computer. We were still obligated to provide the district with lesson plans for our students while on leave, so I wanted to also make sure my students had grades that fairly reflected what they had earned. It never occurred to me that I wouldn't be able to enter my grades.

I was trying to log into my computer from home to address the issue of turning in my grades. Halfway into signing on to my school email account, it actually pixilated away and crumbled off the screen right before my eyes. I briefly saw some of the subject lines before they vanished forever, and they certainly didn't make me feel any better. Some of them were downright vulgar and mean. Since I couldn't email my principal about the grades, I put in a call to the school and left a message for him since it was after office hours. The principal never called me back. We were told that we were not to communicate with each other or any of our colleagues and not to step foot onto school district property.

As teachers, we are expected to extend grace and compassion to students. If a student told me to "fuck off" as they stormed right out of the room after being asked to put away their phone, I was supposed to keep right on calmly teaching and graciously forgive them the next time they came to class. In situations like this, my blood would boil on the inside and the rest of the class would look on in stunned silence as I did my best to continue with the lesson. It's no wonder my body was taking on the stress in the form of sciatic pain.

In the aftermath of being uprooted from our classrooms, there was never a chance to discuss what happened with our principal. We were definitely not extended any grace or compassion. As teachers, we were always teaching our students about online safety and digital citizenship, making good decisions about their online presence. And here we teachers were, branded with digital tattoos. As far as I was concerned, the school missed out on a huge teachable moment for our students. There's nothing like real life scenarios to learn from—but no one wanted to hear what I thought about the situation.

We were plastered all over the media in the most unflattering and despicable way. There we were on the six o'clock news, radio spots, and in newspaper articles. Every single news piece was definitely a one-sided opinion. Not one of us was allowed to tell the story from our point of view. One Southern California news-paper said we had mocked our students. I loved my students and would definitely never do anything to disparage any of them. It was overwhelming.

Luckily, when the administrative leave situation happened and my life started to unravel, I was able to call each person in my family to explain what happened. I wanted them to hear it from me first. I'm glad I did that because on that same weekend right after we had all been banned from our jobs, my parents had very dear friends, Margie and Jerry, visiting from Arizona. My mother and Margie taught first grade together when I was in junior high, and they remained lifelong friends. How sad for my parents to have to explain to them why their daughter was on the six o'clock news and being labeled a racist. Incredibly, everyone in my family—my husband, daughter, brother, sister, parents, aunt, and uncle all stood by my side. They never abandoned me and remained my light through the whole ordeal, which ultimately took about three and a half years to fully resolve.

When some teachers are put on administrative leave, I have heard that they are ordered to report daily to their district office and just sit in a room until the whole investigation is over. Thank goodness that did not happen to us. We did have to provide our weekly lesson plans and call the district office to report in every day before 9:00 a.m. I imagined the secretaries playing sticky note trash can basketball, when they said the same thing every day, "Okay, I'll write it down."

One day at a lawyer's office, at 9:20 a.m. I realized in a panic that I hadn't made my daily call. Heart beating fast, I excused myself and called to report in. "Okay, I'll write it down," was her usual blasé response. Basically, it was like being on house arrest. We couldn't go anywhere because they could call us at any minute to have us report to work.

Time slogged by like molasses, my days and nights blending together into one hazy blur. I was exhausted down to my very soul. I'd lie down to sleep, then toss and turn through restless nights. When I finally fell asleep, I'd wake with a jolt, my head spinning and heart pounding. Or I'd wake up at 3:00 a.m., and just get out of bed since I couldn't fall back to sleep. The delirium of sleep deprivation was definitely starting to set in, clouding my already worrisome view of life.

Never in my wildest imagination did I think I would ever need a lawyer. I was a good, upstanding citizen. Who knew there were so many kinds of lawyers? Certainly not me, but I quickly got an education in that arena. Having no trust in our union lawyers, feeling that they might be too closely aligned with our district, I sought legal counsel elsewhere. Everyone I knew had a lawyer I should check out. It was exhausting and time-consuming. The L.A. Basin (as people in Southern California refer to the region) is pretty widespread with multiple freeways crisscrossing the metropolitan area. I'm pretty sure I traveled them all, logging about 4,500 miles just for legal appointments.

Some lawyers had me fill out huge packets with all kinds of questions about my life. Looking up all that information and filling out all the forms took days. Then I'd travel to hand deliver the documents. Next, I'd wait for a call for another appointment. After finally getting to meet with the lawyer and explain what happened, I'd learn later that they weren't the right kind of legal firm for a freedom of speech kind of case. They all thought my case was pretty innocuous—a "vanilla mom" post. I even had a legal firm from Sacramento contact me. Our First Amendment rights were such a hot button topic in the current political climate, but no one wanted to take my case. The whole situation was disheartening, humiliating, and soul-crushing.

I finally narrowed down my search to a legal firm in Los Angeles, who believed they could cover my case, based on protecting my First Amendment rights to freedom of speech. I had some money, but I still had to borrow from my parents to cover the retainer for my fancy L.A. lawyer. You could see the Hollywood sign from their firm's plush high-rise office. To prepare for my deposition at the district office, I met my lawyer at a Starbuck's near my school. It was kind of funny that I saw a guy and a girl—both students of mine from different class periods—over the lawyer's shoulder. They looked at me quizzically, as I did at them, for they were obviously ditching. This lawyer represented me in my first deposition with the school district.

Unfortunately, that lawyer didn't work out because he wanted more money to answer some simple questions about what the district had against me. He never was able to answer my question about what the school district had against me, so it was back to square one, still looking for legal representation.

Some of my colleagues decided to go with our union lawyers. After all, the cost of legal representation, should the need ever arise, was covered by our union dues. There was a lot of red tape involved in being released from the first lawyer before I was even allowed to speak with the union lawyer who ultimately represented me. It was a long and arduous process just to get to this point. The days turned into weeks, and the weeks into months, and the isolation continued.

My dear, you must be thinking, "How did she go on?" One slow day at a time...going through the motions, to get from one day to the next. When you don't know how to go on, just let yourself be in the present moment. Feel all the feelings. Remember to breathe. Let go, and let God carry you along.

SEEDS TO GROW ON

- *Get in tune with the seasonal flow of life.* Plants go dormant in the winter to renew themselves for spring. Let yourself cycle through, giving yourself to the world then spending some time on you.

- *Be discriminating in your media intake—* online, television, and news. Consider the source to decide if it enhances or diminishes your life.

- *Maintain and nurture the relationships in your life.* When life is filled with turbulence, family and friends can be your anchor. When you spend time with others, put down your phone, turn off the T.V., and go for a walk or bike ride together and be fully present in the moment.

5

WRITE, WALK, PRAY, AND THE REALLY LONG SPRING BREAK

"Come to me all who are weary and I will give you rest."

— *MATTHEW 11:28*

Dear One, I feel your aching heart. You constantly put everyone's needs before you own, sucking your life dry until there is nothing left to give. Sometimes life stops us in our tracks with an abrupt, unshakable message—an earthquake to the soul. The

Universe demands our attention until we get the message that it has something important to say. When you are all the way in the deepest pit of despair, there is only one way left to go, and that is up. So, you start with one step at a time. Put one foot in front of the other, take a deep breath, and just go. Be in communication with yourself and God. Listen to His whispers in the wind. Let Him lead the way.

So, I did the things that led me back to my heart, back to the essence of who I was. Right from the start, with all the empty hours, I wrote. If I couldn't sleep, I'd get out of bed and write. Bleary eyed, tiptoeing to the living room, I'd click on the softest light, get my journal out, and pour my soul onto the waiting page. Unspooling my thoughts, tugging at that thread, I started to untangle the mess my life had become.

Years before, I read a book that resonated with my heart, Julia Cameron's *The Artist's Way.* In it, she speaks of a practice, doing morning pages, where you handwrite three full pages right when you start your day. With my high school teaching job, I didn't see a way the morning pages could fit into my busy schedule, but a door had been opened for me into a wide, expansive land. There was time; I could write. So, I did.

Fast and furious, I poured out my heart, bled right onto the page. I tried my best to capture the craziness that whirled around me. I wanted to remember every detail, as it was all so unbelievable. How in the world could I lose my job over two small sentences I had written, on my own iPad, on my own time, sitting on my couch at home? How was that even possible?

My school district was doing everything in its power to make sure that none of us ever stepped foot into a classroom again. Everything I worked so hard for—my college degree, career, teaching credential, and master's degree could all just disappear—slip right through my hands. No wonder I couldn't sleep at night. My life as I knew it was taken away from me. I didn't know if it could ever go back to the way it was, so the writing gave me solace and a structure to my days. It was a place marker, a starting point, an anchor in the endless days just flapping in the breeze.

I am blessed to live in the mountains in a tiny little village, a secret tucked away in the crowded expanse of Southern California. Just fifty miles from Los Angeles, it is the polar opposite of that vibe. Families here have known each other for generations. It's the kind of place where we chat over garden fences and stick together through fires, blizzards, and floods. There is always someone to lend a helping hand and each person pitches in where they know how.

My grandfather came with his family, all the way from Texas in a Model A Ford when he was six years old and spent his entire life here. Therefore, my family roots are deep here. From where I live now it is literally a two-minute walk "over the river and through the woods to grandmother's house I go." Mt. Baldy and the beautiful home my grandfather built were always home base for me as I grew up all over Southern California with a brief stint in Arizona during junior high. During my ordeal, I had a safe spot in the world where I could slowly emerge from my dark cocoon.

I had to face the music and come out of my house eventually. In the cold of winter, here in the village we tend to stay indoors more so we might not see our neighbors as often. As spring starts to emerge, we make those neighborly connections again.

Since I had so much time on my hands, I walked and walked some more. There are many beautiful places to explore in Mt. Baldy so that's exactly what I did. Plus, I had our lovable Husky mix dog, Dakota, who was always eager to go for a hike around the mountains. He was my confidant and close companion, so good at giving unconditional love. Dakota had the sweetest way of cocking his head to the side when he looked to me, listening to the unbelievable details of my saga.

Sometimes when I was feeling down, I'd go out to his yard and sit on the porch with him. He sensed that I needed extra loving and nuzzled his body next to mine, leaning way into me, almost pushing me over. He'd get me feeling more hopeful about life. He was always so positive and full of energy. Having me home all the time was awesome in his world.

As my faithful pup and I walked around the village and up and down the mountain, we would run into various neighbors. Not having seen me in a while and knowing I taught far away, they'd ask, "Are you on spring break?"

I'd answer, "Yes," to my different neighbors as we emerged from our winter hibernations. That answer sufficed until I started seeing the same neighbors again on different weeks. Curious, they'd look like they were thinking, "Wasn't she just on spring break a couple of weeks ago?"

Although my administrative leave started on February 17, which was super early for spring break, it was now getting to be early spring. In California, school districts have different weeks for spring break, which sometimes makes it hard for families with kids of different ages to plan family vacations.

Eventually, I started having to spill my story of being uprooted from my job. For some reason unknown to me, there have always been quite a few educators living in Mt. Baldy. It's always fun to catch up and compare notes on what's been happening in our classrooms when we run into each other at the post office or on a long walk up the mountain. When I explained to my teacher friends how I had been yanked right out of my classroom, the response was always the same. They were incredulous and shocked that something so dire would be the district's response to our Facebook posts. They were definitely on my side.

My most important teacher friend was always my mother. My parents lived in Long Beach but came to Mt. Baldy almost every weekend. I teased them that they lived like rock stars, living in two places. When my parents came to the mountains, I'd bring them up to speed on what was happening in my case. My parents were my greatest supporters and offered comfort and sage advice. Just a few months prior, my mother discovered she had a rare and aggressive disease: peritoneal cancer. Fighting her own frightening battle, she continued to offer me her love, support, and prayers.

As spring continued to emerge, my daily morning writing and my countless walks with Dakota became my church. They were my doors to constant communication with God. I talked to God and listened. The writing and the walking invited His response. The open silence of the mountain and the blank pages of my journals awaited His reply. I was still up to my neck in nastiness with my school district but being at home in my little mountain village was medicine to my soul. It allowed me to slowly but surely start to fill my cup again.

So, you see, my friend, sometimes we do not know the reason we go through the hardships in life that we do—but God does. When we have the courage to be in the silence and keep moving forward, God will show us the way.

SEEDS TO GROW ON

- *Write out your feelings*—the good, the bad, and the ugly. Try capturing them in your own handwriting as quickly as you can without worrying about grammar, punctuation, or run on sentences. It has been found that there are more neural connections being activated when we write things out by hand vs. when we type. So, journaling in a special notebook gets you closer to the heart of the matter.

- *Walk to create a rhythm to your days.* Go outside and be immersed in the wind, the rain, and the sunshine. Breathe in the air, filling your lungs, and noticing the different scents around your neighborhood. As your feet carry you across the distance, let your steps invite the uninterrupted flow of thoughts. Don't censor or judge what you think. Just observe and let them float by like a leaf on a gentle stream.

- *Connect with your spirit* in whatever way feels natural to you. Start your day by reading inspirational passages. Lift your heart up in prayer. Ask questions to the Universe. Talk to God with every secret concern. Give yourself space to listen. When you tune into what your heart is telling you, you'll find that answers come your way.

6

GROUNDED AND GIVEN ANOTHER CHANCE TO GROW

"Be that one. That One who forgives when deep offense has been committed. That One who loves when no one else does. That One who gives kindness to those who are mean. Be That One who looks past the insult, instead seeing the pain that motivated it. That One who shines light upon those who sit in utter darkness. Because of the impact of being That One runs far and wide. It brings healing to the

wounded, joy to the sad, and hope to those in despair. Be That One."

— SHERI ECKERT

My dear friend, I know you try so hard to be the perfect wife, mother, teacher, friend...the list goes on, we know! You have the best of intentions, and it seems there are just not enough hours in the day to accomplish all that you had planned. I know you have a heart of gold and want to share your love. Sometimes you can be your own harshest judge. None of us are perfect, but we are forgiven when we make a mistake or let someone down whom we care about. Accept the grace that comes with forgiveness and simply begin again. Listen to your heart and start your brand new day.

Though the chaotic ups and downs of my legal case continued for quite some time, I was becoming grounded in uncertainty by sticking with what I knew. My faith in God was unshakable; I never questioned that. I knew in my heart of hearts that I was a good person. It was never my intent to harm another soul. There must have been a reason I had to go through this unfathomable process. I knew without a doubt that my family and friends still loved me. They checked in by calling and sending encouraging notes. I received beautiful and uplifting cards almost weekly from my mom and my aunt Paula. My parents who lived in Long Beach came to the mountains on weekends so they could support me in my case. My husband Alan and our daughter Ashley didn't give up on me either, both steady in their love. My family, my faith, and my mountain tethered me to the world as I went through litigation.

As it turned out, my case was the first to be heard in September of 2017. Before that, the district had a preliminary hearing with me in San Diego during the summer. They tried to get me to walk away from teaching by offering a cash lump sum. That was unbelievable! If I accepted their offer, it would result in a black mark on my credential. I might not be able to ever teach again, even in a different district, if I stopped the case right there by accepting the cash. I decided it was important to fight my case to defend my career and reputation.

Going through the hearings against the district office was one of the darkest experiences of my life. I worked so hard to be a good teacher, even though there were days when I wanted to quit. I never gave up on my students. Despite the varying challenges, I always focused on building relationships with my students. I wanted them to feel loved, connected, and accepted—like they mattered, because they did. If I walked away now, I would be giving up on them. What kind of message would that send? Standing up for what is right is important, so I needed to face the fire of the hearing.

During the hearing, the school district said I was "immoral, dishonest, and unfit to teach." None of those people had ever watched me teach. They tried to make it seem like I was an evil person with hatred in my heart. My accusers did not know that I worked hard to foster a "community of learners" environment, where every individual felt valued. Even more than teaching my students about art, I felt that it was my mission to show them how to be loving and kind toward one another—to build relationships and make friends themselves. I maintained an "open door policy" where students knew they were welcomed at any time. Obviously, these people who were saying such awful things about me didn't know me at all. When it was my turn to speak, I answered their carefully crafted questions, sticking to the truth. I was counseled to not elaborate, so I kept my answers professional and spare.

Grounded in the knowledge that the case was out of my hands, I focused on my faith in God. I was at peace, knowing I had done my part. I hung out with my family, cherishing the time. As it turned out, the gift of time was a blessing. During the same time, my sweet and wonderful mother fought a battle for her life. She was so courageous as she underwent medical procedures for her cancer and watched her body betray her. I spent cherished hours laughing, crying, and talking about life with my parents during that chapter of my life.

As the summer moved into the fall of 2017, one by one, separate hearings were underway for my colleagues. I supported them where I could, attending the hearings until I was asked to leave. I don't think the district liked the fact that I was there with my trusty journal. I thought it was interesting that there were some discrepancies from case to case, in what some people testified under oath. That's not my cross to bear. Still to this day, I would stand up and defend each one of my colleagues, my friends who had to endure the same harrowing process that I did. We each had different outcomes, different timelines, and different things that we "did wrong." In the end, truth and my character held firm, and I finally won my case.

I never did get an apology from my school district. That would have been nice, but by the legal system and the grace of God, I was indeed forgiven. Now it was up to me to let that sink in, forgive myself, and start to grow again. After being out of the classroom for almost a year, I had to prepare myself to work with younger students.

My friend, you might be facing some really difficult challenges in life—rough and uncertain times. Let yourself accept the grace and forgiveness to move forward in life again. We all deserve a fresh start, and we can choose that in any moment.

SEEDS TO GROW ON

- *During turbulent times, let yourself be rooted to the deepest foundations of your life.* Let go and let God uphold and sustain you. Learn to release the outcome in situations where you have given it your all.

- *Accept forgiveness and move on.* We all make mistakes. It's a natural part of life and hopefully we grow and learn from our mistakes. When a toddler is learning how to walk, we don't berate them when they fall. We gently help them get back up and encourage them to try again. Offer yourself the same kindness and grace.

- *Surround yourself with people who nurture your spirit.* Spend time with friends and family who have been with you through thick and thin and still love you despite it all. You know who those people are. They're the ones you can laugh with until your sides ache and tears are streaming down your face. These same friends are the ones who can sit with you in silence when the words have all run dry. Cherish these relationships, for they are golden.

7

BLOOM WHERE YOU
ARE PLANTED

"I've learned a lot this year...I learned that things don't always turn out the way you planned, or the way you think they should. And I've learned that there are things that go wrong that don't always get put back together the way they were before. I've learned that some broken things stay broken, and I've learned that you can get through bad times and keep looking for better ones, as long as you have people who love you."

— JENNIFER WEINER, KELLY'S TREEHOUSE

My sweet friend, I want you to know I'm thinking of you today, sending you light, love, and joy. Whatever challenges you are facing right now, please know that I'm cheering you on from afar. There may be physical distance between us, but I hold you in my heart. I know the dreams you have for your students. You want them all to fly and spread their growing wings. Your own children will be starting to think of college soon and you want the same for them. You want them to discover their passions and make their way in the world.

There's something important I want you to remember. In order to nurture these qualities in your children—be they yours or from another mother—you need to cultivate these qualities in yourself. Let yourself grow and expand, striving for your best. Your students will see and feel your enthusiasm for life and want that for themselves. They are tender young saplings, reaching for the sun. Be curious about life and fill yourself with wonder.

You might be thinking, how in the world can I do that when I'm weary to the bone? You've got to stop. Take care of yourself. Rest when you are tired. It is okay to create healthy boundaries. When you've cared for yourself, you can roll up your sleeves and handle your responsibilities with ease and grace. It's all about pacing yourself and being in the moment—taking mini breaks. It's amazing what a few deep breaths and a quick walk to the restroom between classes can do.

Sometimes, it might even mean giving yourself permission to try something new.

You need to remember to make the time to do the things that nurture your spirit and feed your soul. When I was still at my old high school art teaching job, way before the Facebook fiasco happened, I felt starved for creativity. Here I was, an art teacher, surrounded by creativity, every day encouraging my students to express themselves, but I was not allowing myself the same creative outlet. Sometimes I felt so frustrated that there was never enough time for me, and for the things that I so desperately wanted to create. It almost made me feel like a fraud as an art teacher that I never made any art myself.

Luckily for me, one of my daughter Ashley's friends had a perfect solution. Ashley's friend, Lauren, lived just around the corner from their old high school in Claremont. As a matter of fact, before Ashley learned how to drive, I dropped her off at Lauren's house every day in the wee hours of the morning for two and a half years so I could get to my own teaching job on time. They were both such troopers (along with Lauren's parents) for getting up so early for all that time. Lauren told me that Claremont High School had adult education classes at night and she and her parents, Dennis and Lisa (also teachers), were all signed up for the ceramics class. That sounded like so much fun and they all encouraged me to join.

I am so glad I gave myself that gift of finding a creative outlet again. It was so much fun to be in the ceramics studio, bustling with laughter and creativity. It was fun that it was held in Ashley's old classroom where she had taken ceramics at the high school. Whenever she and her boyfriend, Conner, were in town visiting from Idaho, they even came to class and made stuff. It was perfect that there were no assignments, just a bunch of creative souls having a blast making lots of really cool things. It was like a breath of fresh air being infused into my life, letting myself be creative again. Even though the classes went from seven to ten p.m., which was late for me after my long days of teaching, it was so worth the time, energy, and effort! Going to ceramics and spending fun evenings being creative with my friends made me feel alive again.

So, on a ceramics night, I wouldn't even bother to drag home my heavy teacher bag, full of papers waiting to be graded. I didn't feel guilty at all, not even for a minute. One way or another, everything always gets done. Even if some of the things don't get accomplished, it is not the end of the world. It certainly feels better when you allow yourself the pleasure of doing things that bring you joy!

I'm so grateful that, among other things, I bonded with my mother over teaching. She listened carefully to challenges I faced with various students and offered tried and true advice. When I was teaching, I would often bring over a stack of drawings or paintings to grade as we shared tea and conversation. She would love to see the beautiful drawings and paintings my students created. My parents were so supportive through my whole ordeal and grateful I won my case with the district.

Going through the hearings really shook my confidence to the core. I didn't know if I had the courage to step foot into a classroom again. There I was, starting over again with the grades that had challenged me the most—7th and 8th grade. During my years of substitute teaching, junior high students at schools down the hill gave me a run for my money. They pulled all kinds of crazy shenanigans, making me shake in my boots. That didn't happen at Mt. Baldy School but maybe that was because I had known all the kids and their families since they were in kindergarten. Put me in a room full of thirty-eight high schoolers, and I felt totally confident. At least I used to.

Nevertheless, I had been given a clean slate and a fresh start to be a teacher again. Luckily, I had been able to salvage some of my ten years' worth of personal teaching materials that I developed and accumulated during my time at the high school.

That was a sad day when I was finally let back into my classroom for one day to get my things. My husband, Alan, and Uncle Fred came with me on the appointed day when I was actually allowed on campus. The district didn't want us talking with our colleagues, since we still had pending hearings, so we were given a separate day to empty our classrooms on June 5, 2017.

I would have preferred to do it alone, but I had my family's help. As many husbands are, Alan was in the business of fixing things—that was his love language. My family also knew I was sentimental and had a double curse of saving things as first, an artist, making something of anything, and second, as a teacher, saving materials I could use later in my classroom. Teachers, you know what I mean.

So, Alan and Fred each brought their truck to the school, bringing pile after pile of teaching materials to my desk, saying, "keep or toss, keep or toss," as I quickly made my decisions. It was overwhelming. When our time was up, and their two trucks were full, we had to call it a day, so I was grateful that I at least had some student samples of art projects to help get my new teaching position rolling.

As I prepared myself to start at a new school with younger students, my mother offered this comforting advice, "Robin, just bloom where you are planted." She was right. I knew how to teach and relate to my students. I just needed to dig in and start again where I was.

I always loved getting to know my students and sharing what I learned about art over the years with them. It was so rewarding and validating when students followed my instructions, producing artwork, each in their own unique style. When that happened, at least I knew they understood what I communicated.

Even though I knew these things, I was still nervous to start teaching again after being out of the classroom for almost a year. What if my new students knew what I had been through? I thought I would have students on the first day after Christmas vacation. Luckily, I was given two days in January 2018 to get my portable classroom ready. I felt jittery and unraveled in my new room. There was a constant and high-pitched, ear-piercing buzzing noise. It made my body shiver with its rhythm, and I felt even more nervous than I already was. I couldn't figure out where the annoying noise was coming from. Was it the lights or maybe a speaker? It took a couple of days for the custodian to help me figure it out.

Once I had students, I also discovered that the high-decibel air conditioner came on every five minutes, making me have to shout to be heard. In contrast to the room situation, Mary, my new principal, was really sweet and welcoming, as were the rest of my new colleagues. They were incredibly supportive even though they knew what had happened to me at my old school. Here, the faculty members were very union involved, so my administrative leave saga was a great conversation starter. They were all curious to know what happened to me and offered their sincere support. Since middle schools in our district did not normally have art classes, I was graciously given new students. They had to pull kids from other classes in order to create my rosters. Inadvertently, there was a definite lack of gender balance in my classes. In two of my classes there was one "lone girl" in a room full of adolescent boys trying to "out-testosterone" each other! Talk about crazy shenanigans. There was one boy who happened to be an incredible artist, who kept throwing himself on the floor, and making all kinds of crazy animal noises. That just prompted laughter and others following suit.

Another crazy thing that happened in my portable, permanent trailer classroom revolved around the fact that I was teaching art in a room without water. I didn't want my art students to miss out on the opportunity to do watercolor painting, so my solution was to bring in used, plastic ice cream buckets, complete with bright red handles.

In my mind, the challenge was going to be having the students getting too much water and sloshing it all over the place. To alleviate that potential problem, I had carefully used a Sharpie to mark the two-inch line that they should fill their buckets to. I had it all planned out that the students could go during each class period to get clean water from the restrooms. Everyone was cruising along nicely with their paintings when I noticed one of my "lone girls" not painting. I approached her and asked what was wrong. She answered, "Mrs. Riggle, they got the water out of the toilet." When I saw her gray and swirly water I thought, "yep, you're probably right."

Somehow, with the help of counselors, other teachers, and the principals, things eventually smoothed out as we made our way to May and summer vacation. Another bit of my mom's heartfelt advice was spot-on, too. Since I had always invited students into my room during lunch at my high school, she thought it would be great to eat lunch with my new teacher friends at the middle school every day. She was right.

Teachers always have things to talk about. It is an important break in our days to actually grab a moment to ourselves and engage in conversation with other adults. I was a little bit nervous about joining the other teachers for lunch, but those nerves were instantly calmed. School lunch times are a short thirty minutes, so you have to cram in all the conversation quickly. We talk about our concerns for students we have in common. We ask each other advice about situations we are struggling with. We celebrate weddings, birthdays, baby-showers, and help each other through times of losing loved ones. Teachers can whip up some pretty fast parties in the lunchroom! Being part of a loving and supportive faculty can add so much joy to a teacher's life. It is a shame to not participate in the camaraderie that working together to serve our students can bring. Our shared laughter and conversation in the lunchroom was music to my soul.

So, take heart, my friend. If you find yourself in a situation where you have to start again, it can happen in an instant with a simple shift in perspective. Take a look around you for things you can appreciate. Settle in to where you are. Dig deep, put down roots and let yourself grow right where you already are.

SEEDS TO GROW ON

- *When things seem chaotic and out of control, take charge of what you can.* Your attitude and perspective are always a choice you make. Look from a higher view and remember that your students are young souls just learning to navigate their world. They want and need your guidance, so hold firm in your standards and gently guide them back on track.

- *It is okay and sometimes necessary to ask for help.* You do not have to do it all. Remember that you are on a team, working together to educate your students. Keep parents in the loop and help them set boundaries with their children. Ask your colleagues, counselors, and principals for insights and suggestions when faced with challenging situations.

- *Our classrooms really are our homes away from home*—for ourselves and for our students. *Do what you can to make your environment comfortable and inviting.* Make the effort to dig deep, put down roots, and nurture your relationships at school. Your life will be enriched, and you will find it well worth the effort.

8

WEEDING THE GARDEN

"We need to stop glamorizing overworking. Please. The absence of sleep, good diet, exercise, relaxation, and time with friends and family isn't something to be applauded. Too many people wear their burnout as a badge of honor and it needs to change."

— *@KATYLEESON*

Dear One, I see you putting down roots, growing into your power, and gaining confidence as you thrive. People notice your accomplishments and want you on their team. This is your season of bounty, blooming, and harvest. You are in full production mode, giving your all to your students. Your family needs you more as your teenagers start investigating colleges, learning to drive, and getting starter jobs. You feel alive and energetic as you rush from work to after-school track meets to cheer on your kids and connect with other parents. Don't forget your ever present lesson plans and grading, emails to read and answer, parent phone calls—that's right, remember you have those plans with your own parents this weekend, too. I know sometimes you want it all to stop; not forever, just long enough to catch your breath. I see you need to rest.

That is okay and necessary. It's time to pull the weeds and prune the garden. Cull what is unnecessary and choking fresh growth out. Spend some quiet time to take stock of what is productive and contributing to your life or idling your time. What kinds of things nurture your spirit and make you feel alive? Pursue those things. Learn to say, "No" when you hear your inner voice say, "I wish I didn't have to go" to an event that's one too many. We all get too busy sometimes, and although it might seem hard at first, you really can say "no." Practice it. Look in the mirror when you say it unapologetically. You don't even have to have a reason.

As it turns out, being back on campus with our students "post pandemic" in the fall of 2021, there is a drastic shortage of substitute teachers. All of us have had to pitch in to keep things running smoothly and do "period coverage" and teach another faculty member's class during our prep period. We teachers gladly jump in and help, and I've already given up at least seven prep periods so far this year, as have most of my colleagues. It makes us feel frazzled and like we are behind in the already too long list of things that need to be done.

Sometimes the request to cover another teacher's class comes in the form of an email or a phone call, where you are asked if you can fit it in. I have second period prep and once, as I was about to leave my room after first period, I was greeted at my door with a roster and a request to go teach another class! I didn't even have the time to use the restroom on the way.

So, I have started listening to my needs and have actually said "No" to these requests a couple of times when I absolutely could not fit it in. The school did not fall apart, and my simple "No" was accepted. Listen to your heart and say "Yes" when you can. Absolutely learn how to trust your heart, and if you do not have another ounce of energy that day, it is okay to say, "No, I can't cover that class today." Believe me, your school will keep on schooling all those eager students, even if you did say "No" today.

When it comes to self-care and creating or maintaining work/life boundaries, sometimes you just have to go for the big ask. Our daughter, Ashley and now son-in-law, Conner, got engaged, and we were so excited. Plans were coming along, and Ashley and Conner decided on an August 2020 wedding. In January 2020, they sent out "save the date" announcements, so everyone important in their life would have plenty of time to plan. Then came March and life as we all knew it came to a screeching halt with the global coronavirus pandemic.

During the months that followed, with the pandemic raging around the world, Ashley and Conner tried to make a responsible decision as to whether or not it would be wise to follow through and have their wedding in August. It would have broken my heart to have our only child be married via Zoom. By summer, the pandemic seemed to be simmering down a bit, so the August wedding in the forest was on!

Our school district begins the school year in early August. With the upcoming wedding, I let my middle school principal, Mary, know I would need two weeks off—my year's worth of "sick days" in one fell swoop. I needed the two weeks off since we would be driving to Idaho for the wedding. Mary said I needed to check with the district office on that one.

In my proposal, I let the district know that my need for the time off was incredibly important to me, as this was the wedding of our only child. We needed to drive as we were bringing important items for the wedding. Alan had made a beautiful wooden double diamond "arch" that would frame Ashley and Conner during their outdoor meadow ceremony and provide a view of the gorgeous Boulder Mountains behind them. I was so relieved when the district said yes to my huge request. Time to celebrate! We'd be driving to the wedding, as planned, and I had been granted my two weeks off.

Now my giant job was to prepare two weeks' worth of virtual lesson plans for my middle school art students, whom I'd only known for about a week. I was just barely getting the hang of Google Classroom, myself. I was on a mission, so I dove into making the best ever lesson plans for my new students, so that things could continue smoothly for them. Plus, I shared with my students the reason for my upcoming long absence, and they were excited for me and my family. With the blessing of my school district, I was able to relax and enjoy every moment of Ashley and Conner's wedding festivities—being fully present in each moment—celebrating a big occasion with my family.

For plants to grow and thrive in a garden, it needs to be free of weeds and pests. What kinds of things are sucking energy from your life? Instead of taking home that stack of papers to grade tonight while the T.V. blares in the background, leave them on your desk. I dare you! Instead, go home tonight, grabbing your favorite take-out on the way. After dinner (that you didn't have to prepare), leave the television off and curl up with a book you've been longing to read. Believe me, I have brought home that heavy teacher bag, many times, and have been too exhausted to even grade a thing. Tomorrow you can have your students grade each other's papers, with your guidance, of course. The world is not going to come to an end if you delegate some of your responsibility. You deserve to feel rested and energetic.

Thinking of pests in a garden, sometimes they are just annoying and destructive but have a simple cure. My husband Alan grew up on a farm in Pennsylvania and has awesome skills in the garden. He loves growing tomatoes and often has bumper crops. Tomato worms can wreak havoc and gobble a plant right up. They are wonderful at camouflaging themselves and can get pretty huge if you don't find them early. The tell-tale sign is if you see a tomato plant that is missing lots of leaves near the tips. A couple of summers ago, the tomato worms were quite prolific. I think we even counted about eighty-five or so, over the course of the season. Our dog, Dakota, even got to be expert at sniffing them out. Sometimes he'd be trotting by and spy one we hadn't yet seen and treat himself to some doggy sushi! Yuck!

Where we live in Mt. Baldy is in a National Forest, so we share our home with many beautiful and wild animals, black bears being among them. Anyone who has lived here long enough knows not to put out their trash until the morning of collection, but if you have a tree full of fruit that is ripe and ready to eat, you better watch out. This summer, the bears have been pretty active and feel way too comfortable being close by. Since Alan grew up on a farm, he's had experience with putting up electric fence line. This is the first year that he had to resort to that since the bears would often be up and about all night eating the fruit in our neighbor's trees. Alan managed to save all the peaches, pears, and nectarines from the bears, and they only broke one limb on the nectarine tree.

You might be wondering what we did with all those peaches, pears, and nectarines that Alan was so dedicated in protecting. You definitely do not want bears in your yard breaking apart your trees and tearing apart your garden, so Alan carefully picked all the fruit off the trees as they began to ripen. We had countless five-gallon buckets of peaches, pears, and nectarines in the living room and kitchen for what seemed like weeks on end in August and September.

Alan was born and raised on a farm in Pennsylvania, the youngest of nine kids. His parents were experts at raising everything they needed. When Alan was growing up, the only things his parents ever bought at the store were flour and sugar. Even though Alan watched his mother do canning to preserve all the family's food each year, he had never done it himself.

Alan researched online, figuring out the supplies he needed and picking out recipes that sounded good, combining them to come up with his unique flavors. When you have produce that needs to be preserved, you need to accomplish it on nature's timeline—not your own.

So, here I'd come home, exhausted after a post-pandemic day of teaching in the fall of 2021 and my husband had a kitchen full of peaches, pears, or nectarines that all needed to be washed, cleaned, peeled, sliced, diced, simmered, and stirred—now! All I wanted to do was curl up and take a long, much-needed nap.

But, being a team player, I'd roll up my sleeves, put a towel on my lap (so I could at least sit down), and get out my trusty paring knife and help with prepping the fruit. If you know Alan, you know that he is a hard and dedicated worker and what he does is held to a high standard. Making jam was no exception, so I felt the need to do my part to help, even though Alan was captain on this project.

I'd sit and wash and peel, slice and dice until I couldn't do it anymore. I had to create a boundary somewhere. I pitched in as much as I could, but at 10:00 p.m., I'd wipe off my knife and say, "Alan, I have to stop for the night," and he'd continue on, sometimes until way past midnight. Mind you, I'd have to get up to teach the next day!

On September 17, 2021, I even made a silly post on Facebook about it: "Jammin', we're Jammin', Jammin' on a Thursday night. Midnight, it's midnight, School's just a few hours from now, Sleepin', who's sleepin', Wishing I could get some Zzzzzs." We eventually did accomplish all of that canning and preserving. It really was Alan's project, and I was just a worker bee. I did manage to set a few personal boundaries in there, saying "No" when I had to, in order to preserve some energy of my own.

I had an instance where another teacher at my new school stepped in to help me when he realized something wasn't working for me. He knew my struggles of teaching art in a room that had no water. When he learned that one of our colleagues was changing schools, he immediately let me know. He suggested that I email our principal right away and ask to change my room. Since I was the first to ask, she said yes to my request. Thanks to the thoughtful gesture of my friend, I was able to eliminate what wasn't working for me to improve my situation, and ultimately that of my students. My new room is in a pod where four classrooms share a lounge that has a sink. It also had worn out, thread-bare curtains that were dilapidated and uninspiring. So, I made some new curtains over the summer to make my classroom feel homey and inviting. It was well worth my time and effort as it makes me happy every time I come in my room. When I mention it to the students occasionally when it comes up, my students are surprised that I made the curtains myself and think that it's really cool. They are printed with Walt Disney's original Steamboat Willy cartoon strips.

Any day is an opportunity for a fresh start. We all have things we wish we could improve. Examine closely what isn't working or contributing to the quality of your life. Eliminate what you can. See what new ways of doing and being you can nurture, that will help you feel more alive.

So, you see, my friend, small adjustments, paring things down, finally tackling a big problem, saying no when you need to, or changing a negative habit can all be simple ways of weeding the garden of your life.

SEEDS TO GROW ON

- *Take the time to closely examine what is annoying you or just plain not working anymore.* Look for ways to fix or improve the situation. Sometimes all it takes is just a slight adjustment to make a job go more smoothly.
- *Just say no!* There are times when we really do have too much on our plates—at work, at home, and everywhere we look. It is okay and necessary to stop, take time, reset, and begin again. Don't be afraid to take a wellness day. (This bit of advice actually came from my first principal.) They are built into our schedule for a reason.
- *Let some things go.* That can be anything—habits, clothes that don't fit anymore, relationships, the idea that we have to do it all. Don't feel that you have to grade every single thing that your students write. Take a half an hour one evening to cull one side of your

closet and donate the clothes to charity on your way home from work. Eliminating what no longer serves you can be so liberating and freeing, leaving room to flourish.

NURTURING GROWTH
EVERMORE

"In some Native languages the term for plants translates to 'those who take care of us.'"

— *ROBIN WALL KIMMERER*

Dear One, my sweet friend, are you starting to feel better? You deserve to be happy and enthused about life. Your students look up to you and know you care. Your family cherishes you and wants to see you thriving. Your husband and your children know that they have responsibilities too, because you have shown them that you are creating healthy boundaries. Everyone needs to pitch in to do their part so that no one feels like they are carrying all the weight. Put the things into practice that let you move from just surviving to fully thriving again. You can do it. I believe in you!

Now that I am in my fourth year at my new school, I feel I have gained some perspective. I'm challenged, happy, and wake up eager to go to work and teach my students every day. It is satisfying to look across the classroom and see them all engaged in doing a drawing designed to celebrate their culture.

A great majority of the students in our district and at our school are Hispanic so they are having fun drawing their choice of two still-life set-ups to honor Hispanic Heritage Month. One choice has a Mexican blanket that I bought there when I was thirteen—just about their age—along with an authentic sombrero my grandparents got on a trip to Mexico for my brother when he was only four.

My students love to hear little stories like that because it invites them to share stories of their own. It is interesting how perfect timing can happen in life. My dad, who has always been involved in many community service clubs, recently won a beautiful handmade Navarro ceramic figurine at one of the meetings that he regularly attends. He told his friends that my students would love to draw it, so he gave it to me to share with them, so the statuette, Lupita, is part of their other drawing possibility, along with a beautiful ornamental chili pepper plant, loaded with bright red chilies. I am so proud of my budding artists and the beautiful work that they are creating.

Students are happy and excited to be back on campus after a year and a half of virtual school. That was an incredibly isolating and challenging learning experience for us all. Talk about having to grow! Really, going through the coronavirus pandemic has been something that none of us could have ever imagined and really is a story unto itself.

I have always loved to learn new things and try to instill that joy and curiosity in my students. I feel so blessed to get to grow a garden at the middle school. My husband, Alan, and I have had a garden at home for years and love to grow fruit, vegetables, and flowers. There are eleven small garden plots in a gated area at my school. Curious about it, I asked one of the teachers and he offered me a little plot to plant things in. I have grown various vegetables and flowers in my school garden. Sometimes, I take my students outside for a change of pace so we can draw the garden. Then we have fun with exploring pastels on our drawings.

Decorating the garden for different holidays is always fun, too. Right now, there are flower painted skulls atop candelabras with dangly crystals planted in the dirt to celebrate Dia de los Muertos. Alan had fun helping me engineer a way to attach the skulls to the candleholders so they wouldn't blow away in the wind. He is always willing to help me with school projects when it involves the use of a power tool.

There was a young lady at school who wanted to start a Garden Club, so my principal asked me if I would be interested. One Thursday, we had our first meeting with ten eager young gardeners. When I asked them to introduce themselves and share what they loved about gardening, they talked about beauty, growing healthy things to eat, and getting to watch things grow—all things close to my heart.

Some of them had been fascinated with the sunflowers I grew just for an experiment. During the pandemic, on my one trip to the school in the spring to pick up student artwork for our virtual art show, I stuck a few sunflower seeds in the dirt. Since the plot was irrigated, I figured it would be fun to see what happened. When I returned to campus in early August, I was surprised to see three growing sunflower plants getting ready to bloom—one of them towering way above my head. My gardening enthusiasts wondered where the sunflowers had gone, and I explained that they had finished blooming, and I had taken them out to make room to grow new things. It is an honor to share Thursday afternoons with them and help them to create their vision.

School and life are all about learning and growing. When our students see us wanting to continue learning new things, that enthusiasm rubs off on them. I always make it a point to celebrate and give the students a round of applause, clapping my hands in a circle any time every student is in class. Believe it or not, in my fifteen years of teaching it has not been a common occurrence, so I make it a big deal when it does happen, and I think it inspires the students to try for it again. I tell them that I'm proud of them and that their attendance shows that they are invested in their education. This lets them know that they are important to me, and I care for them. I am here to help them learn and grow into who they are meant to be.

It is always awesome when I can share new things that I am learning with my students. Have you ever had the feeling that something you have been introduced to just keeps tugging at your heart strings the more you think about it? One night while scrolling through Facebook in the fall of 2018, I saw a post about Breathe4Change that drew me right in. It talked about bringing mindfulness and social and emotional well-being into the classroom through their 200 Hour Yoga Teacher certification program. It just looked exciting to me. I had taken yoga classes in my teens and twenties and loved the energy and vitality it brought to my life.

Since long before being removed from my high school classroom, the mounting stress of teaching and dealing with increasing behavior issues took a toll on my body. Sometimes my sciatic pain was so great that it made it hard to stand still in one place for any length of time or even get into my car after a stressful day of teaching. I talked with my doctor, tried physical therapy, received chiropractic care, had acupuncture, and attended Pilates classes for years. I even had to stop taking our Husky mix dog, Dakota, on walks because he pulled so hard. I was running out of options of how I could get to feeling like my energetic self again.

Seeing the posts about Breathe4Change and the yoga teacher training made me remember how much I loved yoga as a teen. I signed up for the January 2019 cohort in Los Angeles and shared my excitement about it with my mom. It was time to take a more proactive approach to my own health and well-being so I could start feeling better again.

As it turned out, becoming certified to teach yoga was one of the greatest gifts I have ever given myself. It was a huge commitment, with classes from seven a.m. to seven p.m. on both Saturdays and Sundays every other weekend from January to May of 2019. Not to mention the one-hour drive into Los Angeles so early in the morning. At least the traffic wasn't bad at 5:30 a.m. on the weekends.

From the moment I walked in the door and started getting to know the trainers and other teachers who were there to get certified, I felt like I was at home. We covered such a wide variety of topics including the history of yoga, non-violent communication, trauma-informed teaching, social justice, breathing techniques, yoga poses, and sequencing. We shared soul-baring activities that helped us build empathy and trust. We created this incredible community together that was absolutely amazing.

As a classroom teacher, I have been able to share techniques with my students to help them cope with stresses they have in their lives. And that sciatic pain of mine is a thing of the past. With yoga, meditation, and mindfulness I learned how to slow down, be in the present moment, and be more in tune with what my body is telling me. It's definitely a gift to feel better and to be able to share these valuable life skills with my students.

So, my dear, if you feel overworked and underwhelmed, you need to take a break. Go out for a walk, get some fresh air, or listen to your favorite band as you dance around your kitchen. Think back to what inspired you to become a teacher in the first place. What is something you have never done, that you would really love to try? Pick up the phone or look online to investigate what you are curious about. Take baby steps. Go slowly at first. Before you know it, you are trying something new.

Ziplining was something I wanted to try. Mentioning it to my sister, Cathy, on the phone one day, she said she wanted to give it a try, too. Nearby options included Wrightwood in the mountains or Catalina Island. Catalina was special to my parents, as they danced and celebrated New Year's there for over thirty years.

On November 28, 2018, as Alan and I celebrated our twenty-sixth wedding anniversary, my sweet Mother lost her battle with cancer and we were all missing her dearly, so Cathy and I thought it would be perfect to include our dad on our adventure and celebrate our mom. The trip became a father-daughter date to Catalina to celebrate our parents' lifelong love. They were married for over sixty years and created a wonderful life together.

As we planned the trip, I thought of my mother and her passing. The day after my mom passed away, I took Dakota on a walk in the pouring rain. It was as if all the angels in Heaven were streaming out their tears right along with me. On our walk up the mountain, I found three heart-shaped rocks—messages from my mom and God—that brought me comfort and peace in the deep and profound loss of her.

As I had gotten into the habit of my morning pages again, one day I shared a journal entry I had written about my mom with my dad. When I read it to him on one of his Sunday afternoon visits, it brought tears to his eyes. He said it was perfect and asked if I could read it during her services. Since she passed away so close to the holidays, we decided to have her two memorial services in January—one in Mt. Baldy and one in Long Beach—both places close to her heart.

I didn't know if I could read what I had written without bursting into tears, but I promised my dad I would do my best. I practiced and practiced, reading as I paced around the house. I must have read it out loud fifty times before I could read it without falling apart. Here is what I wrote:

December 28, 2018, 12:04 p.m.

Even though it isn't morning anymore, I will call this my morning pages. (Maybe more appropriately, mourning pages.) I really haven't written in so long. Today it has been a month since my dear, sweet mother passed away from peritoneal cancer, a rare and very aggressive form of cancer. She was so brave, courageous, and positive in the face of this ugly beast—ever unwavering in her faith in God. Oh! She left big shoes to fill. She taught me to live well and love well. I still have a long way to go to do it as well as she did, though. She truly does have an amazing garden of life-long friends and new ones she has met along the way in the many facets of her life: life-long Mt. Baldy friends, teacher friends, first-grade student friends, (one of whom even introduced me to my husband) who are now grown with families of their own. She has church friends, pool-lady friends, Assistance League friends, Habitat for Humanity friends, tennis friends, square dance friends, book club friends, movie group friends, Kids on the Block puppet group friends, poetry group friends. She had friends I had never even met!

This was not in the "social butterfly, popularity contest" sort of way. Quite the contrary, she was a friend in the truest sense of the word, someone you could sit down and share a cup of tea and conversation with, someone who would listen and actually hear with her heart.

When she and my dad were students at Chaffey College, they were each dating other people and their lockers were next to each other. One day, they looked at each other, after another wonderful conversation, and asked why they were dating these other people, realizing that they were best friends. Breaking it off with the others, they went on their first date on a Friday the 13th and rest was history, sixty plus years of a beautiful life they built together. My parents truly were best friends and modeled such a great way to have a relationship—honest, heartfelt communication, hard work, fun, planning, love, and laughter. Pretty easy recipe when you think about it, but not always so easy to achieve. They sure made it look easy, though. My mother was a doer, one to act, to lead, to encourage, to aim high and reach for the stars, and to help others to do the same. She and my dad started the Long Beach/Los Angeles chapter of Habitat for Humanity right in their living room and recently celebrated building over 1,000 homes with "sweat equity" and volunteers, enabling low-income families to become homeowners.

My mother was a teacher and taught first grade for over thirty years. She was patient and kind and found positive ways to help her students to thrive. Not only did she build relationships with her students, but she also made life-long friendships with teachers and colleagues at work. Since I was born before she was a teacher, and being the oldest of three, I suppose I was her first student. She was such a great teacher! She let us learn by curiosity, fun, discovery, exploration, reading, creativity, imagination, and adventure! Mom and Dad created such a magical childhood for us. We had this thing called "the suggestion box." You could put in ideas of things that would be fun for the family to do together, like go to a park for a picnic, go to Disneyland, go to the drive-in movies in your P.J.s. Sometimes it was even rigged, like when they woke us up super early one morning to draw out a suggestion and it was, "Pack your suitcases. We're flying to California to visit Mimi and Howard!" Yes, she taught us to live life with a sense of fun and adventure.

She also taught us how to learn things on our own. One time when I was nine, my mom had made all kinds of things for the kitchen on her Kenmore sewing machine—curtains, tablecloth, pads for the chairs, placemats, you name it! It was the sixties, and the fabric was bright yellow and orange "flower power" type daisies. She still had miles of fabric left and asked if I wanted to learn how to sew. I jumped at the chance. She showed me her sewing machine and said, "This is forward. This is backward. Yell if you need help." That was in fifth grade, and by sixth grade I was earning money sewing clothes and home decorator items for friends and neighbors.

My parents encouraged each of us three kids to follow our dreams and passions, often in unconventional ways. Not challenged in high school, I took the proficiency exam, finished as a junior and won a full tuition scholarship to fashion design school at Brooks College. Cathy discovered a passion for travel and earned enough money to go to Germany, then later became a foreign exchange student living in Sweden for a year. Michael was discovered as a fashion model, and at seventeen went to live in Paris and on to model on several continents for five years. Yes, my mother was a dreamer and a doer and taught us to believe in our dreams and make them happen, too.

My mother has always had a deep sense of care, respect, and stewardship for the planet. We went on family road trips to go camping in the natural beauty of our National Parks, places like Big Sur, the Sequoias, the Grand Canyon. We were taught that these places (and all places) needed to be protected and preserved. Something she taught us was, "there is no such thing as away," in reference to the way that corporations disposed of industrial waste. (This is something my dad works toward and champions still to this day.) We would go to the drive through recycling center at Cal State Long Beach and get great satisfaction in flinging our bottles, cans, newspapers, and cardboard into the industrial-sized dumpsters. She taught us to take care of the planet and celebrate Earth Day before it was a thing.

My mom's love of nature has been a great legacy she has left with me. I have been blessed to live in the mountain village where she was raised for thirty years now. Alan and I were blessed to raise our daughter, Ashley Dianna, here in Mt. Baldy. She got to attend the same small K-8 school where her great-grandfather, Howard Pruitt, was one of the first eight students in 1921. This is the same school that my mom and my aunt, Paula Pruitt Carter, attended. This is also where my mother started her career as a teacher.

Believing in stewardship and giving back, when her own parents (Marlys and Howard Pruitt) passed, my mom and dad, along with my aunt and uncle, created a scholarship foundation in their honor. This was to celebrate and encourage young people in pursuing their dreams in non-traditional ways. They carried on this tradition for thirteen years.

I would tease my parents that they had a "rock-star" lifestyle, living in Long Beach during the week and in Mt. Baldy on the weekends. And this is not to mention several trips per year to New York to visit my brother Michael and his family. Even being sick with cancer, my mom made these trips with my dad three times this past year. All these visits to the mountains over the years have given me the gift of treasured time spent with my parents. Time spent in conversation, meals shared, ideas tossed around, family celebrations, love, laughter, tears, and hugs. Building relationships was such an important part of who my mother was. Each one of you here today has given her so much light and love and joy. For that, I am eternally grateful.

On the trip to Catalina to zipline and celebrate my parents' love, there's a fun boat ride to get to the island that is twenty-six miles away from the Southern California coast. On a clear day, I can see it as I drive down the mountain on my way to work. At first, Dad was just going to watch us ziplining, but at the last minute, he wanted to join in the fun, too. We all laughed when he told us that he had lied on the iPad waiver form. The age limit was eighty and he was eighty-one at the time.

See, you are never too old to keep learning, growing, and trying brand-new things.

But ziplining wasn't the only new thing my father tried; he and I have also started a new adventure together keeping bees. Since we have wonderful blackberries growing along the stream in Mt. Baldy, it is naturally a great place to keep bees. For three years, my dad had his bee wrangler friend, Clinton, bring his hives up to the mountains to pollinate the blackberries and the many varied flowers growing through the spring and summer. It was a fun venture for my dad and each year, Clinton brought more hives. He shared the honey with my dad in exchange for having a location to keep his bees.

Everything was going well with the beekeeping until the bears discovered the thirty-four (give or take) unprotected hives on my dad's property in the mountains. Clinton thought the bees would be safe from the bears, as they had never disturbed the bees before. The bears tore those hives apart, pieces and parts strewn about the yard, giant claw marks raked across the honey-filled frames. Those bears were incredibly strong, knocking over pallets that had six to eight honey-filled bee boxes strapped to each one. It was a disheartening mess and I felt so sorry for all the bees. The disaster happened in the summer of 2020, such that Clinton did not bring any bees to the mountain this past spring.

Wanting to provide habitat for the bees, as they are so important for the environment, my dad wanted to find a way to continue to support the bees. I heard about a father and son team in Australia who invented a special kind of beehive called the Flow Hive. The idea behind their company and their product is to encourage more people to provide habitat for bees due to the "user-friendly" design of their hives. It is all fascinating and I wanted to join my dad in his beekeeping venture.

We each ordered a Flow Hive kit from Australia. It became a family project, with Alan, my dad, and I building and painting our hives in the summer. The directions said to set aside a couple of hours to assemble your hive. Silly me, I started to put my hive together with my little screwdriver. It wasn't long until I realized I needed to call in expert help. Sheepishly, I asked Alan, a master carpenter and builder, if he could help me. Of course, since it involved the use of all his wonderful power tools, he was happy to oblige.

Since it was already late in the season, and we want to give our bees a chance to really establish their colonies, we decided to wait until next spring to have Clinton deliver us our queen bees and everything else we will need to get our colonies started.

You might be wondering about the bears. The bees will have a protected and fenced in area where my dad kept the bees the first year in the area they were never disturbed. Plus, we'll probably add electric fencing, just to keep those hungry bears away. I'm excited to invite our new bees into their beautiful hives next spring. It will be a learning adventure.

Dear One, by continuing to try new things and exploring things that pique your curiosity, you expand your possibilities in life. It makes you feel more alive and enthusiastic when you continue to learn about new things that interest you. It's also such a great way to model for your students the idea of being life-long learners.

My dear, give yourself permission to grow. What are you passionate about? Follow your curiosities and find things that make you feel alive. Do things you love to do and enjoy every minute. You know you would want these things for your own children and students, so give yourself the very same gift—the ability to find pleasure in life.

SEEDS TO GROW ON

- *Share what you love!* Your enthusiasm rubs off on those around you. I have always loved to garden and enjoyed my little plot of dirt at school. Creating a Garden Club was just a natural extension of what I was already doing. Many hands make light work, and it warms my heart to see the enthusiasm of my young gardeners as we work together to bring their vision to fruition. What do you love to do that you can somehow share with your school community?

- *Follow your curiosity.* What tugs at your heartstrings? Is there a class you have always wanted to take or a place you have wanted to visit? Start investigating and take small steps to make those dreams come true. This is your permission slip!

- *Try new things and be willing to do them badly at first.* Every great rock star, artist, athlete, scientist or engineer was a beginner at some point. It's the trying and trying again that allows us to hone our skills and gain experience and eventually expertise.

10

BLOSSOM CHALLENGE

"The worst thing in your life may contain seeds of the best. When you can see crisis as an opportunity, your life becomes not easier, but more satisfying."

— *JOE KOGEL*

Dear sweet teacher friend of mine, as I sit in my garden at home in Mt. Baldy on a breezy October Sunday afternoon and write this final letter to you, my heart is filled with gratitude. I have so enjoyed our correspondence and the insights I have gained. My sincerest hope is that you have enjoyed them, too.

Can you feel the calm, wide-open space as the wind whispers through the cedar trees? Do you feel the warm October sun caressing your back as you memorize the moment? I want you to realize that you are perfect, just the way you are. You were created in love, so you can love yourself. When you do, a world of possibilities opens up for you. As I pen these final thoughts to you, I want to offer a B.L.O.S.S.O.M. C.H.A.L.L.E.N.G.E. I want you to believe in your dreams and grow into the best version of yourself that you can be.

So, you might be thinking, just exactly what is a B.L.O.S.S.O.M. C.H.A.L.L.E.N.G.E? It is a new way of thinking about words. In the King James version of the Bible, John 1:1, it says: "In the beginning was the word, and the word was with God and the word was God."

Many people don't realize the power that our words have in creating the lives that we live. We have the God-given power to choose our thoughts and our thoughts create our words. I let my students know every day that they are responsible for their words and their actions. When they carefully observe their thoughts and words, they can create more positive outcomes. I want the same for you, Dear One.

So here is my B.L.O.S.S.O.M. C.H.A.L.L.E.N.G.E to you. I envision the acronym to mean, "By

Letting One Self Soar, Opportunities Multiply," and C.H.A.L.L.E.N.G.E. to mean, "Continue Heightening Achievement Levels, Learning Everything Needed, Gaining Experience."

Here is what I wish for you: that you blossom fully into who you are meant to be. Every thought you think and word you speak draws experiences into your world. By following your desires and curiosities, you are nurturing your soul. They were planted in your heart for a reason. As an acorn grows into a majestic oak, a tulip bulb grows into a flower in the spring. If we let ourselves naturally unfurl into the world, we will be in alignment with our truth. When we can learn to listen to our heart's true urgings, we soar to the greatest heights. Instead of swimming upstream, we can flow with the river of life, so believe in yourself. Let yourself bloom into who you were meant to be. You just might surprise yourself when things start to flow your way. The Universe pulsates with infinite abundance, and you are an integral part of the ebb and flow of life.

"So, what about the Challenge part?" I hear you wondering. When I think about the essence of the word "challenge," here's what comes to mind: To live life to the fullest, we were designed to reach and grow, stretching higher for greater achievements as we master each new skill.

As my brother, Michael, likes to say, "We are all just students in the University of the Universe." There are levels and layers unfolding step-by-step. Everything we ever needed is already there for us inside our hearts just waiting to be discovered. Life is about learning. Learning is about discovery. Our needs have already been met. All we have to do is claim them. With everything we do and try in life, we gain a new experience.

Get yourself some sunshine, some water, and some rest. Be sure to throw in some nourishment and God can do the rest. Life keeps on "life-ing." Believe in yourself and become the best that you can be.

SEEDS TO GROW ON

- *Be present in the moment.* When we let ourselves fully engage in the ever ongoing moment of "now," we will feel the richness of life. Take the time to meditate, if even for only a moment. Stop and notice everything around you—sights, sounds, scents, sensations, and tantalizing tastes. We live in an amazing world. Remember to pause every once in a while to take it all in.

- *Blossom into who you are meant to be.* What are your greatest yearnings? What wishes do you hold close to your heart? What do you love to do? What makes your heart sing? Give yourself time and space to truly think about these things. Little by little, take the steps to move into closer alignment with your authentic self.

- *Challenge yourself to keep on growing.* It has been said that if we are alive, we still have work to do. The nature of all living beings is to reach, stretch, strive, and grow. Dear

One, this is my greatest wish for you: By planting these seeds and letting them grow, may you finally find a balance that lets you flourish, grow, and thrive, both at work and at home. May you find your place in life that truly lets you *bloom where you are planted.*

With Love,
Robin Reed Riggle
Mt. Baldy, California
October 3, 2021

11

STILL BLOOMING,
THRIVING AND
MOVING THROUGH
THE CHALLENGES

Dear One, I still see you. It's been a long time since we've been in touch. I wanted to let you know that I'm still learning, growing and evolving as an educator. I hope that you have been able to navigate these past few years in the classroom and find your way back to some sort of normalcy again, too.

Actually it's been four and a half years since first releasing my book. You are right. The past few years in the classroom and on campus have been a crazy ride. We (mostly) survived the global corona virus pandemic. All of us, some more than others, have experienced trauma from this experience. If not directly ourselves, most of us can probably name someone who lost a loved one.

In the world of school and education, the whole way of teaching and learning had to pivot in an instant due to the threat of the deadly virus. I remember coming onto campus that first summer in 2020, to get some of my teaching supplies during the height of the pandemic. Arriving at school and stepping into my classroom was like being in a ghost town that had been vacated rapidly. "Friday, March 13, 2020", was still written on the white board and stacks of student artwork were still covering the counters. Who knew it would be nearly a year and a half before we were (kind of) back on campus again?

Those first weeks back to school were tenuous at best, with teachers being paired up to share a classroom to consolidate the "deep cleaning" of the room between the blue groups and the orange groups that shared the space. Monday and Tuesday were for one group and Thursday and Friday were for the other group, with Wednesday being set aside for "sterilizing" the classroom. There were even stickers on the desks for where the orange group students should sit and blue stickers for the opposite group of students. The sidewalks outside had 12" stickers plastered everywhere reminding students and staff to "maintain social distancing", in other words, to stand six feet away from each other. It was kind of unnerving when someone would get "in your bubble" and stand too close to you, especially if they had their mask dangling from their face, not even bothering to cover their nose and mouth! Don't even get me started on the mask thing. I know doctors, nurses and dentists have been wearing them for ages, but teaching and having to talk all day with a mask on was difficult at best. Being able to hear students clearly was really hard, too. It was a bummer having to wear my glasses for things like taking attendance. Having to repeat names several times in order to be heard clearly across the room, only made my glasses more foggy. Not only was this hard at the start of the new year, but the masks made it a real challenge to memorize new student names quickly, too. Some students had long hair hanging down over their eyes with barely a sliver of their eyes visible above their masks, giving me very few identifying features to learn about them. I hated the way my exhaled air made my breath feel stale and awful by the end of the day. The whole thing was exhausting.

I wasn't going to complain about something so silly as having to wear a mask all day, though. In the throes of the COVID pandemic I had my family. I had food on the table. I got to be at home in my beautiful little mountain village. I had the shortest commute ever. I literally walked the block and a half, "over the river and through the woods, to grandmother's house I went", to my grandparents' house, that my father still owns. I got to do my virtual teaching in my mother's childhood bedroom, in the beautiful home that my grandfather built. No one I knew had gotten COVID. I had a job to do—taking care of my students. During the worst of the pandemic, when we all had to learn to teach from home via computer, I really felt that my most important job was to just love my students. Very few students signed into the virtual classes with their cameras on. Some had logos in place of a photo of themselves—things like LA Dodgers, Sponge Bob Square Pants or other cartoon characters.

Technology is an area of my life where I am still learning and growing, and it's definitely not my strongest skill. Unlike my students, I did not grow up with computers. Luckily our school district had things set up to pretty much, "plug and play". My school issued computer definitely did not have enough spunk to be connected to 35 students at a time, let alone our sluggish internet in the mountains. The lack of good internet at home played a part in the decision to work from home at my grandparent's house, since it had way better internet, provided by a local carrier. Pavel, the owner of

Baldy Connect internet, was just a text away, should I have any technology issues. There were a few times that my students got to meet Pavel online, when he came to save the day. It was also a benefit to have a separation between my work-space and my home life. The first couple of days with my virtual students were a disaster. Neither my camera nor my microphone worked on my school computer, so I literally had to type instructions for their art assignments in the chat box to the side of the "Brady Bunch" array of student icons (or black circles). I went out and bought myself a MacBook Pro, and things definitely took an uphill turn from there!

In addition to the importance of just being there as an emotional support for my students, I made it a safe space to cobble together some sort of comforting virtual community. Some students were quite vocal, easily speaking into their microphones and sometimes even showing themselves on camera. Some students were excellent communicators via typing in the chat box. Some students signed on every single day and never said a word, nor did they ever turn in an assignment. I think some students just got a certain sense of comfort from "being together" online. I tried my best to offer love and support by asking each of them how they were doing and checking to see how their families were doing. It's interesting how pets and other animals became an important part of our classroom community. Some students had dogs or cats with them in their bedrooms or at the kitchen table, so we got to meet their pets. Some kids took us on their morning rounds to feed their chickens or their horses. There was even a student who sometimes had a bird sitting on his shoulder. One afternoon, to the delight of my students, a mama deer and her three fawns strolled by in front of my window. The deer family was there long enough for me to grab my phone and make a short video to share with them. Though he was never seen on camera, my students knew we had a beloved dog, Dakota. As part of our conversations online, many of us shared fun stories of silly things that our pets did.

Continuing with my philosophy of having my students feel like, "I see you" as being important, I made it a daily habit to check in with them and see how they were doing. Students were learning how to reciprocate the idea of seeing how I was doing, too. We had been together as virtual classes for a couple of months and there was a certain comfort that came with being together online as we checked in on each other during the uncertainty of the pandemic. Sadly, our sweet and lovable dog Dakota had gotten cancer in his bones over the summer. With our virtual classes, we had class periods in the morning then afternoon classes after a nice lunch break. I usually walked home for lunch during my break. Dakota, being pretty rambunctious, had been an outdoor dog for his entire life. With his sickness my husband and I agreed that Dakota deserved the comfort of being indoors, just in the living room. On this particular day, Dakota watched me intently from the garden, as I walked to work to begin my teaching day. I had given him a big hug before I left, as was my usual custom.

Later that afternoon, when I waked in the front door for lunch, I saw that Dakota was lying on his side near the coffee table. I reached down to give him a little love pat and felt the last little bit of his life flutter out of him. It took me by surprise and I burst into tears as I told Alan, "I think Dakota just passed away". It was heartbreaking. It is amazing how our pets love us so unconditionally. We definitely have something to learn from our animal companions when it comes to loving others without an agenda.

Suddenly pulling myself back to the present moment, I realized that I had to return back "to school" and teach my afternoon virtual classes. My eyes were red, tears were streaming down my cheeks and I could barely catch my breath. I had to pull myself together, and quickly. In the virtual teaching world, there were no substitute teachers to come and save the day—especially not with five minutes notice! Alan gave me an encouraging hug, and off I went to my grandparents' house to try and teach my afternoon classes.

Once in my workspace in my mom's old bedroom, I signed onto my virtual classroom and one by one my students signed on, too. They each greeted me with friendly, "How are you, Mrs. Riggle?" questions. Quietly, I told each student who asked that I was feeling sad today and that when we were all in the "classroom", I would tell all of them the reason why, together.

With all of my afternoon students present, I took a big breath and through teary eyes, I told them that my sweet dog, Dakota had just passed away during my lunch at home. In what should have been an incredibly sad conversation, I found myself feeling flooded with love and gratitude. My students uplifted me with their genuine caring and support. One student said that they had brand new puppies and would I like one. My chat box was flooded with comments like, "we love you, Mrs. Riggle", and "we are so sorry". I do not remember what the art lesson for the day was even supposed to be about but I will never forget the outpouring of love I felt from my students in that moment. (I am crying now as I write about this experience.) Somehow as our world was falling apart around us in the craziness, loss and sorrow of the pandemic, here was a golden moment of teacher and student connection that I will treasure forever. Love and compassion was at the root of it all. More than anything, these were the kinds of lessons that I most hoped to teach my students, and here I was, being the recipient of their love.

As teachers we are used to walking around the classroom all day long and connecting with our students. A really challenging part of pandemic teaching was the never-ending sitting in front of a computer! Every part of my job was done while sitting in front of my computer—lesson planning, teaching, grading, staying "after school" and documenting individually for all 150ish students their synchronous and asynchronous attendance, communicating with students and parents, answering emails from administration, and figuring out how to do art lessons with the reality of most students having no art supplies at home. There were some fun results of having to rethink the way I taught my virtual students about art. When we were learning about color and the color wheel, I doubted that all of my students had colored pencils at home. I suggested that they go on a scavenger hunt around their homes and gather things in all the colors on the color wheel. They could arrange their objects in a circle with the colors in the appropriate places and take pictures of their results. When it came to doing portraits, I told my students to practice drawing their siblings while they were watching TV or to draw their pets while they were sleeping. If they turned in their portrait on a piece of lined paper torn out of a notebook—no problem—at least they had given it a try. There was way too much sitting! I couldn't wait to go outside to get some fresh air and go for a long walk up the mountain. I definitely needed to go recharge my batteries.

As the months of pandemic teaching slogged on like molasses, and the mounting global death rates continued to be announced on the nightly news, our virtual classrooms fell into a rhythm of their own. Just chatting with my students remained my highest priority. We learned some things about art but we learned more about life and coping and loss. I had students who got COVID or lost loved ones to the virus. Art was definitely not the most important topic in the "room".

Eventually we all made our way back to campus, after about a year and a half. That's when we had the orange and the blue groups. Even though they called it being back on campus, it hardly felt like real school. We still had our virtual classes online. The back to campus part was really just for Advisory/Homeroom class during the spring semester and it was voluntary at the discretion of each family. I had two or three students signed up and my pandemic partner teacher had just about the same amount of students. Some days I would make the hour drive to school and none of my students were in attendance. There was only an hour break between in person school in the morning and the afternoon virtual classes. This wasn't enough time for my commute home and getting my computer set up for virtual classes. So I had to stay on campus to do my virtual classes. This time felt a lot like I was spinning my wheels, emotionally and realistically in my car!

After that one semester of easing back onto campus (just barely) the following fall we were officially back to school. We all had our masks, gloves, Clorox wipes and 3'x5' Plexiglass shields in front of our desks to prevent the spread of the deadly virus. Being back on campus with our students was almost like being in the Wild West. Students were not used to spending time together with their peers. Walking onto campus in the mornings and crossing the quad, it was evident that none of the students were interacting with each other. They were all staring at their phones playing video games or texting each other instead of talking with their friends. Largely isolated from each other during the pandemic, these kids had actually not had the opportunity to just hang out together as friends. They had lost or never learned the valuable skills of communicating feelings, negotiating differences, and just laughing and having fun together with their buddies.

In the classroom, this played out in some extreme ways. One student raced around the classroom grabbing baskets full of colored pencils, and threw them around the room. Sometimes wild and obscene profanities were blurted out loud enough for everyone to hear. As the teacher in scenarios like this, the other students need to see that you are calm and doing your best to handle the situation. The lesson for the day suddenly becomes last priority. In a case of wildly disruptive behavior, I usually ask the student to step outside for a few minutes to calm down, so that we can later have a private conversation at the doorway about the offending behavior. Most students can usually pinpoint what they did to get sent out of the room. I'll ask them if they are ready to come back into the room and try again. Sometimes students will take me up on the offer to share a few deep-breathing exercises together. In extreme cases like the flying pencil boxes or large group art projects getting ripped off the wall, it is definitely all right and necessary to ask for help from the principal. The principal arranged for the students who caused these huge messes to come in during passing period or lunch and repair the damage they had done. An important message that I have always relayed to my students is that they are responsible for their thoughts, words and actions and that they need to learn to make good choices. The classmates who sadly have to witness these extreme events need to see that we are fair and consistent in our expectations so that we may provide a safe learning environment for everyone. Working through some of these difficult challenges just meant that we were all learning how to be together in person again.

As educators and school organizations we need to demonstrate that we are lifelong learners and open to change that will improve student outcomes. There have been some positive school wide outcomes as we have made our way to a greater sense of normalcy following the pandemic. Being aware of and sensitive to students' social and emotional wellness has gained attention as a priority. Providing a safe space for students on campus, with our new wellness center has helped them to acknowledge their feelings, ask for help and learn valuable coping skills. Our school was lucky enough to receive funding to address this issue by creating a P.A.W. (peace and wellness) room that provides much needed services to our students. As the center was being designed and built, the director of the program asked if my art students could help create a sense of student ownership and belonging for the space by designing calming mandala watercolor paintings to be displayed there. The wellness center has been a tremendous addition and a much used space on our campus. Students who might be having an off day or just need a bit of encouragement can ask to take a 15 minute break to check in with one of our wellness center counselors. When they return to class they have a renewed sense of calm and a readiness to try again. Now in its second year of operation, the student wellness center continues to be a huge success in providing these important resources that help students learn to cope with challenges and regulate their emotions.

Another positive outcome following the pandemic was that our school decided that we wanted to rebuild a sense of community both on campus and beyond. The demographic of our school and district is largely Hispanic. To honor and celebrate the culture of our community we created a new tradition that would be meaningful and have relevance to them. For the past two years we have had a campus wide Dia de las Muertos celebration, both of which were incredibly successful. When we first started with this big dream, everyone was on board and actively engaged in preparing for the big day. We invited community members to participate by making booths and displays about their programs or businesses. The parent booster club got involved in helping with the preparations. Groups on campus like AVID, ASB, Band and Choir were all looking forward to the big day getting ready for what they were going to contribute to the festivities. As the art teacher, I had lots of fun making opportunities for my students to create art revolving around the theme. I showed them the movie, Coco so that they could draw their favorite scene. Two different Ofrendas, (altars in the home, honoring ancestors who have passed on before us) were set up in the classroom as still life set-ups for the students to draw. There was another fun project that we did. I explained that at their age, they might not have ever lost a loved one yet. We were going to draw memorial portraits. Instead of drawing someone they had lost, the students could choose someone they admired to draw. The portraits turned out beautifully, done in white colored pencil on black paper, they had a classic timeless feeling to them—perfect for the subject matter. I was amazed at the beauty and attention to detail that the students showed in drawing and painting lovely artworks to be displayed at our celebration. On the day before Dia de los Muertos, we were all busy in the multipurpose room getting everything set up. When it all came together it was so lively, colorful and amazing. There were gorgeous orange marigolds everywhere. The students' beautiful artwork adorned the walls. Flower arches and Ofrendas of all colors, shapes and sizes were on every table. Students could have their faces painted or make colorful flower headbands. Our Band and Choir classes provided musical entertainment. There were even spirited and colorful Ballet Folklorico performances done by students who attended the high school where I used to teach. This past year we even added food trucks so everyone could enjoy the delicious flavors surrounding the rich traditions of the celebration. Though I am not Hispanic, I really enjoyed celebrating with the students and their families as we bonded over sharing stories of loved ones we have lost. It was definitely one of those days where we all looked around us and took in the hard work and dedication that went into creating this event and collectively agreed, it was worth it and we all did a great job. Hopefully it will be a new tradition that our school continues for years to come.

As I am contemplating things that still have meaning for me as a teacher, I am drawn to four words: consistency, connection, communication and change. Each of these concepts is relevant and important in building strong relationships with your students. Working with kids and building relationships with them, where they know that they are safe to try new things, has been at the forefront of all the time that I have spent in the classroom with my students. That is where the richness and the moments of joy and discovery can be found.

What I still know to be true is that kids need consistency, in other words they need guidelines, expectations and boundaries. I am strict on certain things, for example my "no phone" policy. As I greet each student at the door before each class period, I ask that they put their phones in a zippered pocket of their backpack and leave it there for the entire class period. Phones can be a huge distraction and since the brains of young middle school students will not be fully developed for several years to come, they are not yet able to make some of those decisions that are in their best interest. On their behalf, I do my best to advocate for the sanctity of the classroom environment by requesting that they not use their phones in my classroom. Students do not always comply and when that happens I request that they bring their phone over to my desk drawer and let them know that we will have a conversation about phone use after class. I need to do this, to let the students who follow the rules every day, know that I uphold my classroom guidelines. Students need to know that school is a place where learning should be taking place away from the temptations of texts, social media and playing endless video games. These kinds of things should definitely not be going on in the classroom and I am the one who needs to uphold those boundaries. I recently heard that on the average, people spend approximately 7 ½ hours a day on their phones! Surely that is even higher for some people. We need to model what we expect our students to do. It's a double-edged sword. Phones can be amazing tools. Look at all the incredible things that they can do: calculate math, take photos, keep your calendar, text friends, watch You Tube videos, call people, look up any subject imaginable... the list is endless. You as an educator need to decide how you want to approach phone use (or not) in your own classroom. I know that at my school, some teachers allow students to use their phones in class. That inconsistency from class to class, makes is difficult sometimes to maintain those expectations. Our school district gives each student, from Kindergarten to 12th grade, Chromebooks to use for the duration of their enrollment. I include the use of technology in my lessons by having the students do research on their Chromebooks, where they have access to all the information that they need.

As a check on my own phone use, I have recently started making my lunchtime more mindful by keeping my phone put away while I eat. That way I can focus on enjoying my food and being more fully present in the moment. This is definitely a way I can relax and recharge my batteries between classes full of energetic teenagers. This way I prevent myself from mindlessly gobbling down my lunch while I doomscroll. Instead of doing something that depletes my energy, I can return to my classes with a sense of calm and preparedness. Actually I do not have my phone out during class at all. I check for messages anyone might have sent me after I am done eating or at the end of the school day.

Another thing that I still believe, is that one of the most important things you can do as a teacher, is to make connections and build relationships with your students. Ask them about their lives. See what makes their eyes light up. When you share snippets of your own life with them, it invites them to do the same. It is important to share with your students that you re continuing to grow as an individual, following passions, curiosities and interests (where appropriate). Let them know when you accomplish some of your dreams. Just recently I shared with my students that after three years of beekeeping, my husband and I finally got our first harvest of honey. This year we got not only one, but two honey harvests, after making sure that our bees had more that enough honey for their own needs. When I talked about how much my husband and I loved gardening, one girl who learned we were beekeepers, eagerly shared how much she loved to garden with her grandmother. When I told my husband about this student, he suggested that we put together a little package of seeds and things from our garden to share with her. This young lady was so excited to receive a variety of flower seeds, succulents and a tiny pumpkin from our garden that she could share with her grandmother. I later learned that she lived with her grandmother because she had recently lost her mother. Even though I never shared with her that I knew of her mother's passing, as I learned of it in confidence, I could still hold this girl in my thoughts and prayers and have a greater understanding of the difficulties she was facing. It never hurts to extend a little kindness and compassion towards our students. We just never know what challenges and difficulties our students are faced with. You also never know what seemingly insignificant little thing that you do might open the door to an invitation for connection. I sometimes write little messages to loved ones when I write the date for the next school day on my white board—things like "Happy Birthday Alan" and "Happy Anniversary Paula and Fred". Just the other day on May 9th, I had written in tiny letters, "Happy Heavenly Birthday, Jeannette". I had forgotten that I had written the message when out of the blue a young man in 5th period asked me, "Who's Jeannette?" I wracked my brain for a moment before I remembered what I had written on the board at the end of the previous day. Jeannette had been a dear friend when we both went to college at Chico State in Northern California. Sadly she passed away after a medical mistake left her in a coma during exploratory surgery for a minor problem. I was able to share with my student the happy memories that we shared together in college and then about her unfortunate passing. He then shared with me, that he had lost a cousin in a drive by shooting. This fleeting conversation with one of my students opened the door to a deeper connection and greater compassion for this young man in my class. Look for those moments. Be open to them. The little conversation that you have with a student on any random day just might not be so random. Leave the door open for those exchanges that might not be about your subject matter.

Clear communication is still at the top of my list of important things that I strive for as a teacher—across the board—with students, parents and colleagues. Say what you mean and mean what you say. In communicating with your students it's important to find moments where you can let your students know that you are proud of them. I recently found such a time. I jotted this down in my journal on April 29, 2025 at 9:51a.m.

I'm sitting in my classroom filled with my 8th grade Advisory students as we are in the third and final week of state testing. This is not usually a favorite activity for them. This has been the most quiet and respectful group of students I have ever administered state testing to. One student is still taking the test and everyone else is being patient and quiet. Sometimes in a testing situation the students are like popcorn, popping out of their seats and making all kinds of noise when they're done. Not this group! I have been sure to thank them and let them know how great they have been at giving it their best effort and following the strict guidelines. Students love to know when they are doing well and simple praise on a job well done goes a long ways in building their self-confidence. You can see the pride glowing in their eyes when you give them genuine compliments.

Clear and open communication with parents is of utmost importance, too. My mother, a first grade teacher with over 30 years of experience, shared this with me. She reminded me that a "good student" parent phone call is worth its weight in gold. Parents are so surprised and full of emotion when you call them, introducing yourself as their son or daughter's teacher, and you let them know what an excellent student and polite young man or woman their child is. Call when their child has made huge improvements or if they have done something kind for a student who is being bullied. Sadly, it is often the good, polite and quiet students who go under the radar and are unnoticed. Make the effort to compliment these students. Tell their parents they are doing a great job of raising a hard working and polite child. It is sweet to see these kids the next day when they enter the classroom, walking just a little bit taller. In contrast, it is just as important to call a parent if you are having behavior issues with their child. Perhaps something is going on at home that has changed the situation in the classroom for the student. By reaching out to a student's parent you can gain a greater understanding of the full picture. If a student is repeatedly being defiant and undermining your authority in the classroom, that student's parent definitely needs to know about the situation. If possible at the start of a conversation like this, begin with something this student is doing well or find something to praise about them. Ask the parent what you and they can do together to help the student get through this phase. Show them that you are willing to work together as a team to help their child grow. Along with clear communication to the parents of a student who is misbehaving, you also need to clearly communicate with your colleagues about what is happening. Perhaps other teachers are having similar issues with the same student. Then it might be time to let the school counselor know what is going on and schedule a parent teacher conference with all of the teachers. Make it an important task to accomplish, even if you have to stay a few minutes later after school, to document in a way that is appropriate for your school setting, the series of behaviors and actions taken to try and remedy the situation. This way you are covering your bases, should there later be a need for further discipline for this student. If you forget to do this step, perhaps the student will not be placed in the situation that is best for his or her progress. Remember to clearly communicate with everyone involved in any given situation—even people in the future who would benefit from having all the facts clearly documented.

Lastly I have been thinking about the word change. Life is about change and without change we would not exist. Change is about growth and expanding our horizons. We all definitely learned that to get through the global pandemic, we needed to completely change the way we interacted with and taught our students. We had to be open to change to move the learning environment to the virtual world. When the pandemic was of less danger we had to be open to learning how to be together as a community of learners again on campus. Education policies, strategies and buzz-words are always changing. Students are always changing as they move from childhood into the greater independence of adolescence and beyond. As their teachers we need to help our students find a sense of stability in an ever-changing world.

It's funny that as I'm thinking about all the change that goes on in the world, some things never change. Some students will always feel the need to deface school property with swastikas, write foul things on desks, break brand new colored pencils and throw them across the room. I jokingly tell my students that in my 18 years of teaching I would be a millionaire if I had a dollar for every penis drawing that I have come across in my career. Why do kids do that? And what's up with the flying carrots? Sometimes during the afternoon classes, after coming in from lunch, some students feel the need to throw baby carrots across the room. I really am a loving, kind and fair teacher. It baffles me as to why these annoying behaviors happen. No matter how diligent I try to be with my classroom management, some things still fly under my radar. This is all just proof that even with all of my classroom experience, I still need to be open to change, growth and learning new ways to tackle challenging student behaviors.

Today's students grew up in a different world than we did. They are digital natives. I walked to my neighborhood public library after school to check out books to do the research for the reports I had to do in school. Our students today have every fact in the universe tucked away in the phones that are always within an arm's reach. Every year I have been a teacher, I have had my students make Earth Day posters. I tell them that they will be the future leaders of the world and that we all need to be good stewards of the planet. I have them learn about problems that we are faced with on a global level and I also have them research solutions to these problems. As part of the preparation for this project I used to go to the public library and bring a couple of bags of large coffee table books filled with gorgeous photos of things my students could research for this project. I do not do this any more. The last straw was when I was returning the books and saw that one of my students had torn out a page with a beautiful photo of a gorilla. I was horrified that one of my students had done this on my watch. I offered to pay for the damages and the librarian insisted that they had archivists who knew how to repair such things. That was the last time that I spent my time, effort and energy bringing those beautiful books to school for my students to use. What I have learned is that many students just don't want to look at books anymore. They want to just instanta-neously find whatever they are looking for with a few swipes of their fingers. As educators we need to be open to change the way we deliver our lessons. I have learned to be flexible and welcome the opportunity for my students to use their Chromebooks to research ideas for their projects. Yes, life is full of exciting changes and as a teacher who still loves to learn new things, I am eager to see what the future of education holds in store for all of us. When I taught at the high school I used to joke with my students, when we were talking about the rapid advancement of technology, that I was waiting for all of us to just get USB ports in our belly buttons. We would be able to instantly download any information that we needed.

My hope as a teacher is this—that we can all leave the world a better place than we found it. As a teacher I try to instill the idea that we are each responsible for our thoughts, words and actions. We all need to make good choices in life. I believe there is hope for the future. As teachers we have the privilege of helping students learn to navigate an ever-changing world. We also get to play a small part in encouraging them to believe in their dreams. Though some days of teaching are so hard that you want to walk out of the classroom in the middle of a class period, other days are filled with so much hope and so many wins that you remember why you started this journey as a teacher in the first place. It is truly an honor and a privilege to get to work with other people's children to teach them not only about the subject that you love, but also to teach them, day by day to become the very best versions of themselves. My dear teacher friend, it is my hope that you find joy and inspiration in the stories that I have shared with you. I want you to remember how wonderful you are and what a great teacher you are. Your students need you to be in charge of their classroom as a kind and consistent teacher. You've got this! I believe in you.

SEEDS TO GROW ON

- Always remember to nurture yourself, reserve some time just for you, and follow your passions and dreams. Make this a regular thing in your schedule each week. That way, no matter how demanding your school week has been, you have something fun or meaningful to look forward to and you can return to work refreshed and have the ability to serve from a full cup.

- Sometimes it's ok to laugh with your students and let them see you being silly. I have an alien antennae headband that I got on a family road trip last summer—aliens had become the unofficial mascot of our cross-country trek. Anyway, this headband ended up in my classroom and I sometimes wear it just for fun. When the students walk into my room and they see me wearing the silly headband they know they can be themselves, too. One of my Master Teachers, Mr.

Nyberg had an awesome rainbow Bozo wig in his supply closet that he sometimes threw on just to lighten the mood. When there is joy and laughter in your classroom, that is when the magic of learning is at its finest.

• As The Beatles so famously said in their song, "All You Need Is Love", that idea pretty much sums up my philosophy of teaching. Love yourself first—enough to always keep learning and growing—modeling what you want your students to do. Like they say when airplanes take off, put on your own oxygen mask first, then you can help take care of others. Love your students in a nurturing, caring and encouraging way. Sometimes one of my students will ask me, "Am I your favorite student?" I answer by telling them that I love all of my students. And this, my dear is true. I love you, too because you have dedicated yourself to one of the most meaningful callings you could have ever chosen.

Dear Teacher Friend of Mine,

In closing I'd like to share this final thought,
"Don't be afraid to say Yes! to your dreams.
God put them in your heart for a reason."

With Love,
Robin Reed Riggle
Mt. Baldy, California
June 1, 2025

ACKNOWLEDGMENTS

As an author there is an amazing invisible exchange with other people once you put your book out into the world. On a recent day when I came home from work, my husband Alan told me with excitement that someone had called me about my book. That person was Literary Agent, Benjamin Lopez who wanted to help me republish my book so that it could reach a broader audience. As part of this journey I decided to write an additional chapter reflecting back on the past 4 1/2 years since first releasing my book. I also wanted to include interior book reviews that I wasn't able to accomplish the first time. Benjamin, thank you for believing in me and my story. It is my hope that with your help, my book will be able to offer help, inspiration and encouragement to teachers (and others) around the world.

To my dear friends who made time in their busy schedules to write heartfelt reviews for my book, I am filled with gratitude. I am humbled by the kind words that you all had to say about my story. Thank you to: Nida Wanthivanond, Patty Van Osterhoudt, Jeannine Dole, Nancy Sirski, Toni Fletcher Blackmon, John Norvell, Lisa Cook, Rhiannon Wamsley, Pat Montague, Ikzury Paneto, Jessica Reed, Harvey Slater, Linda Sanchez and Rebecca Park. Most of you are teachers and we just made it through another school year! I hope you all get a chance to relax, have fun and recharge your batteries over the summer.

It's a mysterious thing to have a relentless urge to write a book about a profound and life-changing experience. It can seem like an insurmountable task. Being a life-long journal keeper, I wrote my heart out, capturing all my feelings from the moment I was yanked out of my classroom.

Julia Cameron, thank you for giving me the tool of morning pages and journaling to carry me through the dark times and back into the light. I love your book, The Artist's Way, and the positive impact it had on my life.

Cindy Blackstone, thank you for inviting me into uncharted territory and helping me sign up for a Facebook account during our lunch break all those years ago. I didn't want anything to do with social media since a student had earlier created a fake and vile

Myspace account, complete with a photo of me in my classroom. But you assured me of how worthwhile and fun it could be.

Despite all the pain and suffering having a Facebook account brought into my life, I still believe that social media can be a positive force in the world. Without Facebook, none of this ordeal would have happened. I also would have lost out on all the growth and change that happened in my life because of my participation in that Facebook thread on February 16, 2017. I have always tried to post positive, uplifting, and inspiring thoughts, photos, and ideas on social media, especially since I am a teacher. I deeply apologize to the people I may have hurt with my words. To hurt anyone was never my intention. Mark Zuckerberg, thank you for bringing Facebook into the world. Look at all the exchange of ideas and connections you have facilitated.

As a matter of fact, it was through Facebook that I found the invitation from Dr. Angela Lauria and The Author Incubator to finally write my book. Thank you and your expert team for guiding me on this journey and never giving up on me, even when I wanted to give up on myself.

Karmi Koen, from the moment of our first talk, I felt welcomed onto the team by you. Thank you for your sparkle and joy.

Ramses Rodriguez, I loved every call I got to participate on with you during the summer. Thank you for sharing your wisdom and humor with all of us in a positive, no-nonsense way.

Marianne Williamson, thank you for so graciously sharing your positive and uplifting spiritual guidance with us on Wednesdays. I appreciate your calm and steady presence.

I would love to thank Jennifer Stimson, who designed the beautiful cover for my book.

Thank you to all my fellow aspiring and accomplished authors I have met and been inspired by on this journey. You know who you are. You have both extended and answered the hand of friendship and I treasure each one of you. Thank you for all the encouragement and cheers!

Madeline Kosten, I would like to especially thank you for your gentle guidance through the daunting editorial process. I love your constructive criticism and the way you break things down into steps I can cross off my huge to-do list. I couldn't have done it without you.

To my teachers along the way in life—you are all amazing! From my first day of kindergarten, sitting cross-legged on the floor looking up at the alphabet, uppercase and lowercase, marching across the wall on their chalkboard green background, I knew I was at home. I knew those letters. I knew those letters made words. I knew those words told stories and painted pictures in my brain. All the way to my graduate level classes, each teacher I have had in my life contributed to who I am today. I thank you all for that.

If you are a teacher, I especially want to express my gratitude to you. Thank you for answering the call to take on this important and often thankless work. It takes patience, kindness, tenacity, hard work, sacrifice, love, dedication, and so much more to be a good teacher. Thank you, teachers, for all that you do in service for your students.

To my Master Teachers at Upland High School, Boyd Nyberg and Liz Aurilia, thank you both for being the most amazing teachers and sharing your trade secrets with me. I am forever grateful for the way you welcomed me into this important profession. I learned that music and laughter can go a long way in building relationships with our students. "Let's open up the studio" was Boyd's cheerful way of starting class for the day. And I still have my students mix their own colors when doing colored pencil assignments, thanks to Liz's inspiration.

To my colleagues at my former high school, I always considered you family and the school our home away from home. Thank you for helping me become the teacher and person I am today. Keep up the good work of preparing our students to spread their wings and fly in the world.

To my fellow Facebook fiasco teachers—to this day, I consider each of you my friends. You are excellent teachers. We are forever bonded by the harrowing experience we faced. I wish you each happiness and peace in all your endeavors.

To Carlos Perez, I am forever grateful to you for representing me in my case against the district. Even when I sought legal counsel in all the wrong places first, you defended me in your calm and gentle manner. You preserved the integrity of my credential and my character, and it is due to your guidance that I won my case and protected my career. Thank you from the bottom of my heart.

To my colleagues at my new middle school, thank you for welcoming me with open arms and helping me to believe I could teach again, even when I didn't think I could. I appreciate the fact that you are union involved and advocate for the rights of teachers. I love that together we are instilling *Habits of the Mind* and *Habits of the Heart* into the lives of our young students.

To Dr. Ilana Nankin, thank you for founding the amazing organization, Breathe4Change. Getting certified to teach yoga and bring mindfulness into the classroom was a profoundly moving experience.

To Carole Tokudomi, my longtime friend and hair stylist, we have traded stories and friendship over many years. Thank you for helping my mother to feel beautiful as she prepared to leave this life. I always feel like a new person every time I see you. Did you notice that in my photo on the back of the book, my hair looks awesome thanks to you?

To my community of Mt. Baldy village, thank you all for making this such an incredible place to call home. We are all so blessed to live here. For me, having such deep family roots here influences so much of who I am. It makes me strive to be a better person.

Thank you to my grandparents, Marlys (Mimi) and Howard Pruitt and Marianne (Mernie) and Harold Reed. You are all long gone from this earth, but your love lives on in me. Howard, remember when someone would ask you one too many questions and you'd say, "You writin' a book?" Well, guess what, I did! Mimi, I always feel your spirit, whispering in my ear, "If a job's worth doing, it's worth doing well." Mernie, your love of doing crossword puzzles inspired a love of words in me. Grandpa Reed, a railroad engineer, I feel your call to adventure when I hear a train whistle sound as it rolls on down the tracks.

To my aunt and uncle, Paula and Fred Carter, I love you dearly and cherish our times together. Having no children of your own, with you in our corner, it has always been like having an extra set of loving parents for me, Cathy, and Michael. Paula, thank you for never giving up on me. All the beautiful, uplifting cards you sent helped me through the turbulent times. Fred, your steady and practical outlook helped me to realize the storm would eventually pass.

There's no greater love than that of siblings and I'm blessed with two of the best. Cathy, you were always the early bird to my night owl. I loved when your flute music floated out your bedroom window, down into mine, and wove its way into my lazy summer morning dreams. Michael, my fellow "Cosmonaut," I love that we share that same twisted sense of humor. I can always count on you to find the laughter, even in the darkest of times.

To my parents, David and Diane Reed—thank you for the gift of family and unconditional love. You raised each of the three of us to find our passions in life. Our shared conversations over the years taught us compassion, belief in ourselves, and stewardship for the planet. Mom, you were such an incredible teacher, and you inspire me to do my best for my students. Though you've been gone almost three years now, I am encouraged by the messages you send me from the spirit world. Thank you for all the heart-shaped rocks you put in my path so often.

Dad, thank you for setting the example of being a dreamer and a doer. You showed me that where there's a will, there's a way. First you were a minister, then a financial planner and now your next dream is becoming a reality, turning trash into hydrogen fuel. You have always worked so hard to make the world a better place. I am so excited to see where your businesses, Clean Energy Enterprises and Clean Green Energy Machine, take you next.

To my husband, Alan—thank you for making my dream of having a family come true. You are hardworking, a man of integrity, and a great father to our daughter, Ashley. You stand by me through the ups and downs of life. Thank you for always challenging me to be the best that I can be. I would love to thank our daughter, Ashley Dianna. Born on your grandpa Riggle's eighty-ninth birthday and named for both grandmas—Anna Geraldine and Diane, in your middle name—I loved you before you were even born. I have loved every minute of getting to be your mom. Your dad and I are so proud of you and Conner and the life you are building together. Thank you to Cissy and Pat Madigan for raising two of the finest young men on the planet, Conner and Aaron. Thank you all for continuing the bond of love and welcoming Ashley into your family with open arms.

All of my thanks and gratitude go to God for making this beautiful, crazy, inspiring, and wonderful life possible.

With much love,
Robin Reed Riggle

ABOUT THE AUTHOR

Robin Reed Riggle is a fourth-generation Californian and has lived just about half of her life in Mt. Baldy, a tiny village nestled in the mountains of Southern California. She and her husband, Alan, raised their grown daughter, Ashley, there. The K-8 Mt. Baldy School has been a focal point of Robin's life for generations. Her grandfather, Howard Pruitt was one of the first eight students to attend when it was established in 1921. Later, Robin's mother and aunt attended there. Then her mother, Diane Pruitt Reed, began her thirty-plus year career as a first-grade teacher at the little two-room school.

Robin's first venture into the world of teaching was as a parent volunteer at Mt. Baldy School while Ashley attended. Gaining confidence in the classroom, Robin became a teacher's aide and later a substitute teacher. After subbing at Mt. Baldy School and the Upland Unified School District for about six years, she decided she wanted her own classroom. She holds a bachelor of fine arts degree in illustration from C.S.U., Fullerton. She earned her single subject in art teaching credential and master of education degree from University of La Verne. Robin also earned her 200 Hour Yoga Teacher and SEL Certification through Breathe4Change.

She has taught art to both high school and middle school students for the past fifteen years and loves to help each of them find their own creative style. Robin and her husband love to camp, hike, garden, and visit their daughter and son-in-law, Ashley and Conner, in Idaho.

PHOTOGRAPHS

In my high school classroom doing Christmas still-life.

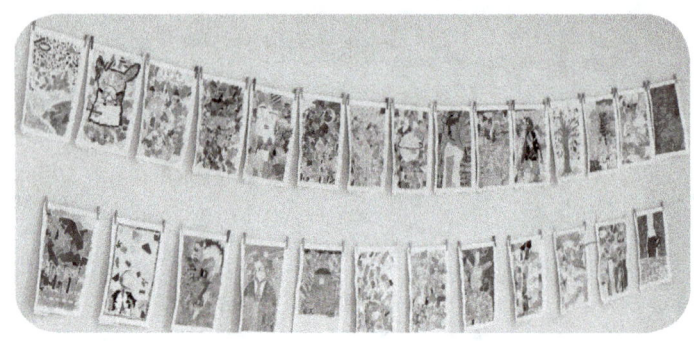

Middle school art show display of student collages.

*My watercolor painting for middle school
art show: peony from my garden.*

Ashley, Alan, and Robin—a surprise snow in Mt. Baldy.

Alan, Robin, Dakota, Conner, and Ashley
on an autumn hike in Mt. Baldy.

Ashley and Conner's Wedding and the "Really Big Ask"—
My district granted my request for two weeks off so we
could drive to Idaho for our daughter's wedding.

Alan and Robin with their first honey harvest after three years of Beekeeping—so many fun things to learn about taking care of bees!

Making connections with the community—our school wide Dia de los Muertos Celebration

GIFT FOR READERS

Thank you for reading my book and taking this journey with me. Being a teacher in today's world can be so challenging and yet so personally rewarding. As teachers, we are giving by nature, and it can be so easy to give of ourselves past the point of resilience. It is my deepest hope that you have been able to learn from some of my experiences. In sharing my story of how I became a teacher, despite plans of my own, I found that I was truly called to this work. There is a special kind of satisfaction that comes from making connections with students that really help them to believe in themselves.

I hope that I have been able to offer you help and encouragement when you have felt that you can't continue being so burnt out from teaching. My wish for you is that you learn to believe in yourself again, too. Perhaps through using some of the tips I have shared to create a stronger work/ life balance, you will be able to find ways to truly blossom in all the areas of your life that are important to you.

If you would like to reach out with any comments or questions, I can be reached at: robinreedriggle1@gmail.com

Currently, with my full time teaching I do not have a formal Facebook group for this book, but that could be a future possibility. Until then, find me on social media.

LinkedIn: Robin Riggle
Facebook: Robin Riggle
Instagram: robinbobobbin2019

Wishing you all the best,
Robin Reed Riggle